PRAYER SUMMITS

PRAYER SUMMITS

SEEKING GOD'S AGENDA FOR YOUR COMMUNITY

Joe Aldrich

MULTNOMAH

Portland, Oregon

Unless otherwise indicated, all Scripture references are from the Holy Bible: New International Version, copyright 1973, 1978, 1984 by the International Bible Society. Used by permission of Zondervan Bible Publishers.

Edited by Steve Halliday
Cover design by Bruce DeRoos

PRAYER SUMMITS
© 1992 by Joe Aldrich
Published by Multnomah Press
10209 SE Division Street
Portland, Oregon 97266

Multnomah Press is a ministry of
Multnomah School of the Bible
8435 NE Glisan Street
Portland, Oregon 97220

Printed in the United States of America.

Library of Congress Cataloging-in-Publication Data
Aldrich, Joseph C., 1940-
Prayer summits / Joe Aldrich
p.   cm.
ISBN 0-88070-422-5
1. Prayer groups. 2. Clergy conferences. 3. Church renewal.
I. Title
BV287.A45   1992
264'.7—dc20   92-15259
                                                                          CIP

92 93 94 95 96 97 98 99 00 01 - 10 9 8 7 6 5 4 3 2 1

Contents

REUNITUS: The Possible Dream

Do prodigal brothers and sisters ever come home?

Like prodigals we've clipped coupons on our inheritance and distanced ourselves from our roots back at the ranch. With a modicum of success we've built our own kingdoms, deified our traditions, and staked out our turf. All without concern for dad or elder brother.

But when our best meals start tasting like corn husks, isn't it time to look up from the trough? Isn't it time to "come to our senses," spread out the road map and journey homeward toward reconciliation, restoration, and revival?

What is it about unity that seems so distasteful?

Jesus prayed for it, but we've yet to see it happen. In fact, what's happened is just the reverse: the house of God has become a broken home. And broken homes don't work. Divided houses don't stand. Disunited churches forfeit their redemptive effectiveness.

Broken homes have little to say to a broken world.

I wonder—could the fragmented family of God be reunited around its heavenly Father? Or is our Lord's prayer for unity merely divine rhetoric?

We often say, "If it isn't broken, don't fix it." But what if it's broken? Is there a way back home?

- Can the family recover its power?
- Can God's people become a triumphant army once again?
- Can they shake their world as did our forefathers, the first century church?
- Can a reviving, renewing work be initiated and sustained in specific geographical areas?
- Could the true Church in your city ever come together and be the Church?

Reunitus may be the key that unleashes the corporate power of God's diverse family to stake claim to the streets and neighborhoods of countless communities. It could ignite a divine firestorm; it could lead God to command his blessing upon repentant churches. Revival could be right around the corner.

So what's so special about the Latin word *reunitus*?

This significant term comes from a root which means "to make one again, to bring together again."

It challenges the divided to join hands, the distant to draw near, the dissenting to seek reconciliation.

It calls us to restore unity, a quality so important that:

- if marriages had it, divorce would be virtually nonexistent.
- if families had it, we wouldn't need juvenile detention centers.
- if nations had it, we wouldn't need to stockpile weapons or maintain vast armies.

Mankind longs for it. The success of marriage, family, church, and government depends upon it.

It's so important, unseen principalities and powers expend immeasurable amounts of spiritual energy to oppose or counterfeit it.

If the Church ever caught it, your neighbors and mine would hear the music of the gospel in a most convincing manner. Churches with it would:

- see the Lord add "daily to their number those who are being saved."
- qualify for the blessing of God.
- find favor with God and man.
- significantly impact their communities.
- see whole cities impacted in concrete, measurable ways.
- fulfill the John 17 mandate.

Its presence would silence the critic and attract the unconvinced. Its presence would release large amounts of spiritual energy. Remember, where it exists, God commands his blessing (*see* Psalm 33). When present, unity scatters hope in every direction.

Its return would be a miracle.

Friend, we're talking about UNITY. Not uniformity, not even union, but unity.

Couples divorce when they believe they are no longer one. Families fly apart without it. Lacking unity, nations rise up against nations, churches split, denominations compete, elders feud while pastors fume. And whole cities remain under the control of the Evil One.

Is it any wonder we're commanded to pray, "Your kingdom come, your will be done on earth as it is in heaven"? The rule of God among men is extended when his children bow to his agenda. His will on earth is done when we live together in unity. The flow of spiritual energy is blocked, and the coming of God's kingdom is hindered and delayed when believers oppose or ignore each other.

Mark it well, friend. In the spiritual realm, a "cold

war" is perhaps more insidious than outright battle. The Latin root of insidious means to "lie in ambush." It suggests covert activity, not visible, frontal engagement. Caricature and innuendo are effective cold war weapons. It's the "Well, yes, but . . . " syndrome. Maybe you've heard it:

"Well, yes, Pastor Smith loves the Lord, but . . . "

"Well, yes, those people believe in justification by faith, but . . . "

"Well, yes, you can be Christian and sprinkle, but . . . "

"Well, yes, Charismatics can be Christian, but . . ."

"Well, yes, the Bible does teach us to anoint the sick with oil and pray for them, but . . . "

"Well, yes, the psalms talk about raising hands in worship, but . . . "

"Well, yes, there are other versions besides KJV, but . . . "

"Well, yes, but . . . Well, yes, but . . . Well, yes, but . . ."

Mark it well from the start. Unity isn't coming to agreement about these kinds of issues. In the light of a lost world on its way to hell, they're inconsequential. The stakes of unity are much higher. The very redemptive plan of God is at stake.

Disunity surfaces when eyes tell hands, "We don't need you." Or ears tell eyes, "We don't belong to the body." Or one prides oneself in being a follower of Paul rather than of Apollos. If the body doesn't function properly, if unity is missing, Paul reminds us, it will not build itself up in love.

In Search of the Missing Link

Is there a missing link? Absolutely. It's unity. Adam and Eve lost it for us in the paradise of God. Driven from Eden, polarized by sin, crippled by selfishness, the first couple quickly discovered disunity had taken up residence in the very the core of their beings. Their kids came down with it and Abel died at the hand of his brother, Cain. A lethal dose of disobedience laced with a pinch of jealousy was all it took to precipitate the first murder.

To murder is to take life away. It can be done in an instant or over many years. The process is over when vitality is gone.

Disunity is slow-motion murder. Like a trapped fly in a spider web, we fight its destructive momentum for a while and then finally succumb. We lose hope, we give up and toss in the towel. And hell chalks up another victory.

When turmoil comes, when cracks appear, the majority opinion is to separate, to go our own way and so:

marriages end.

dreams die.

ministries split.

we become accomplished fugitives from God, ourselves, and others.

Christian communities forfeit their corporate impact.

Cities lie in the control of the Father of Lies.

But it gets worse. We not only separate, we become competitors for the grace of God—as though he would grace our diseased communities with fresh, new babies. For those few riding the crest of spiritual affluence, ignorance is usually bliss. Comfortably situated, these brothers and sisters see little reason to participate in the needs of the churches in their community. In fact, not a few would consider such efforts as compromise (often a handy label for what we don't understand). At best we ignore others who name the name of Christ—unless, of course, they are of our particular denomination.

Is it any wonder the non-Christian is unimpressed with our platitudes?

A Fixed Point of Reference

I'm told that most satellites are designed to lock onto a star as a fixed point of reference. As long as they are targeted on this reference point, they are able to function as designed. The success of the mission is dependent upon staying permanently fixed to that assigned luminary.

Isn't that what unity is all about?

To have unity is to function according to divine specifications. When husband and wife are locked onto God as their infinite reference point, unity is possible. His agenda for them is that they become one. Surrender to that agenda is necessary, though not easy nor automatic.

God is the ultimate reference point—the place where the cosmic buck stops. God has the final word on every issue and every subject. When you've tapped into him, there is no higher court of appeal, no higher standard, no rival. Every thought, Paul reminds us, is to be brought into captivity to Christ and Christ alone.

God has only one agenda. If pastors and elders seek only the agenda of The Ultimate Reference Point and set aside their own, unity is possible. If the cry of each heart is, "Your kingdom come, your will be done," there is no room for competition.

If churches, cities, counties, and whole countries bow before His sovereignty, whole cities can repent and lands can be healed. It's happened in the past.

Could it happen in our generation? What is our role in bringing it to pass? That's what this book is all about.

What Is Unity?

I suppose that the Memorial Coliseum full of rabid Trailblazer fans is about as close to complete unity as we'll get apart from an act of God himself! True unity has a core focus that is sufficiently powerful to overcome the gravitational pull of self-centeredness and greed.

There are many things which bind people of every stripe together in common cause:

For bankrobbers, it's the promise of wealth and possessions.

For athletes, it's the possibility of an Olympic gold medal or a Super Bowl ring.

For a military commander, it's ridding the world of a dangerous enemy.

For the businessman, it's reaching the top.

For the pastor, it may be the pathway to building a mega-church.

For the mature believer, it's the Divine agenda.

For the spiritual leaders of the community of faith, it is the maintenance of a united front.

Unity is crucial in most arenas.

It's a topic of conversation that surfaces frequently and in all kinds of environments. Most enterprises see it as vital to their success. The seminar circuit is loaded with sessions devoted to team-building. Teamwork is a recognized component of achievement.

In the New Testament, unity is exalted as the ultimate evidence of spiritual maturity. Churches that have it are recipients of God's approval and blessing. Without it, churches curl up and die.

Where disunity prevails, something is seriously wrong; its presence should trigger a flashing red light on our spiritual dashboards. If you don't think it's a severe problem, try building a successful, thriving enterprise around low staff morale. Paul tagged the Corinthians as carnal and worldly because of their constant quarreling and jealousy (1 Corinthians 3). They lacked unity! You remember the circumstances. They were trying to rally around people and personalities rather than around the corporate purposes of almighty God.

Paul encouraged the Ephesians to be diligent to "keep the unity of the Spirit through the bond of peace" (Ephesians 4:3). Maintain unity, Paul says, between yourself and:

God;

your marriage partner;

your family members;

your church leadership;

your church family;

your community.

What does it take to reverse the tides of enmity and strife and become the people of God? Can the united, networked Community of Faith bring about change in their towns and cities? Is it possible to "take a city," or is Nineveh's repentance an atypical, once-in-a-lifetime event? Is it possible to restore churches and ministries wracked with division and strife? What does it take to experience a revival of God's power and blessing upon a diseased ministry? A diseased marriage? A diseased community? A divided church? A city under Satanic siege?

Is it possible to begin and sustain a movement of God in your community? In my community? The answer is yes. The question is *how?*

The following illustration may give you a clue. Taken from a pastor's journal, it records how God used a Prayer Summit to profoundly touch over sixty pastors from Northern Washington. Dozens of other groups right now are experiencing the same revival. In this book we will consider both Prayer Summits and Solemn Assemblies. As used in this book, Prayer Summits are conferences designed to bring about renewal and unity among pastors and other church leaders. Solemn Assemblies, building on the Old Testament model, are specially called assemblies designed to address disobedience and sin in the congregation of a local church.

This account of a Prayer Summit will give you a flavor of what God is doing throughout the Pacific Northwest and beyond. What changed the lives of these pastors can work for all who are serious about impacting their world for Christ. Certainly it illustrates the "engine" of revival, the beginnings of the healing and empowering of the church.

One Man's Breakout

June 1, 1990

So much has happened the past few days. I've been to heaven and back and can't wait to record it all here.

For months, a number of pastors and Christian leaders in our area have been anticipating a "Pastors' Prayer Summit" together. On Memorial Day, we all loaded in our vans—-about sixty men in all—-from the towns of Kitsap County to go up to Warm Beach for the much anticipated happening. And a caravan it was indeed. Charismatics and Baptists, Church of Christ and Episcopalians were all heading in the same direction!

On Monday afternoon, we began four days of prayer together. Not one message was given (that in itself is a miracle among sixty preachers!).

From the very first, God began to move in incredible awakening and reviving power. It was to be one of the most precious seasons of awakening that I have ever experienced in my life.

The first day focused on loving and worshiping Jesus and renewing our relationships to Him. We would sit in a large circle with about two rows of seats and simply go to prayer. Some would lead out in song. Some would share a Scripture. All would pray—listening to each other and building on the previous petition. Most of us had never met before. It was amazing to see God begin to melt our hearts together as we made the simple commitment to love Him and share our hearts.

The first evening, the showers of awakening were already in evidence. Trust was being built among the men. We had begun to pray for one another. As the sun set, we gathered around three small tables to share communion. Soft candle light brightened the warm conference room. As various men knelt to receive the elements, the group led forth in the thundering praise of many of the great hymns of the church. We were falling in love with the Savior again. We were growing to love one another.

On Tuesday morning we met again after breakfast to seek God's face. His agenda was the only one that mattered. This day he began to lead us into the heart of revival: humbling ourselves before one another in confession of sin. Sometimes a chair would be placed in the center of our circle and men would voluntarily come to the front and "share with us the gift of their need." Tears began to flow freely as men shared their hearts, allowing others to minister to them. Some were bound in the chains of lust. Others were struggling in their marriages. Some had grown up in the homes of alcoholics and were reaching out for love. The variety of needs seemed endless.

Yet, the response was always the same. As a man would share his need, other brothers from the audience would make their way to the front to pray for and encourage the one who was baring his soul. Prayers flowed like healing waters. It was so tender and yet so intense that it was almost impossible to get your prayer in. You had to be fast! Man after man came to the "hot seat" in front and went away built up and encouraged by the intercession of the saints. Hugs and tears were becoming commonplace. God was making us "one."

During this time, an Assembly of God minister stood to confess his sin of judgment toward a Conservative Baptist minister. With tears in his eyes he said, "I was told in Bible school that you believed all the wrong things. I thought that you were elitist. Now I see that I was wrong. You love the same Jesus. You believe the same things. Please forgive me."

The Baptist pastor then blurted out, "I thought the same things about you. But I was wrong. Would you forgive me?"

The two of them then crossed the room and hugged each other as the tears flowed freely. They didn't just fall from their eyes. All of us in the room were being instructed and forever changed.

In the evening we had one of the most moving communion times I have ever participated in. As I watched the flow of prayer, praise, love, and unity simply envelop the inhabitants of the room, now aglow only with candlelight, the thought struck me, *This has got to be what the Upper Room experience must have been like in the Book of Acts following the death and resurrection of Jesus.*

That seemed the most appropriate comparison. Out of brokenness and prayer and a zeal for God, a great depth of unity and vision was being born.

We were staying in a lodge that overlooked the beach. Late at night the men would still be fellowshipping, talking about the things God had done during the day. In the morning hours before breakfast, men would be all over the two hundred-acre property. Some would walk on the beach and pray. Others would slip off into the myriad woods for a quiet time with the Lord. I spent my morning quiet times singing and praying to God at a beautiful private amphitheater that overlooked the Warm Beach coast.

Following a wonderful breakfast, we began the third day of the dealings and healings of God. This day God led us to focus more on our relationships to our wives and also to our ministries. The format was still the same. God put the agenda together. As the Spirit would lead, men would come to the

"hot seat" to be prayed for. Precious times of intercession, laced with encouragement from Scripture
and the ever-present "pastors' choir," would lead to
victory in the lives of the leaders. Love and unity
continued to grow. Its depth appeared to be limit-
less. Many themes were prayed over:

•A black pastor shared his burden over racism.
Many white brothers knelt with him and embraced
him in the Lord.

•A leader of a parachurch ministry shared his
desire to not be divided in any way from the
strengths of the local church. This led to a wonderful time of prayer for ALL of God's ministries to
flow together, not in a spirit of competition, but in
a complementary spirit of cooperation.

•An Episcopal minister shared his burden for some
Roman Catholic leaders who were unable to
attend. We prayed that they would be with us the
next time!

And there were even some moments of holy hilarity.
During one time of prayer a pastor commented,
"As the leaders of God's church, we've all been
sick! It's time to get well, and to lead the flock on."
We all laughed together at our new-found unity in
weakness and sin. The walls that divided us were
coming down. This was a wonderful reality, but
also a scary responsibility. Where would it all lead?
Only God knew, and as Gene Edwards says, "He
never fails."

The final night we broke off into our various town
groupings to share the elements of the communion
table. Hours went by as we ministered the bread

and wine to each other. Every man was prayed over individually, and together we committed ourselves to never be the same again. We were now going to be the best of friends. We were going to live out the unity that is found in Christ and demonstrate its power to our communities.

The final morning we gathered to worship God and to sign a covenant. In it we committed ourselves to the Lord, to one another, and to revival in our towns and nation. We also made some specific commitments:

•To meet together weekly in our various towns for prayer for revival and for one another.

•To get together monthly from the whole county to fast and pray and seek God's face for the welfare of our area.

•To draw our wives into the same experience with the Lord in brokenness and fellowship.

•To hold another Pastors' Prayer Summit for an expanded circle of men within a year's time.

•To schedule an area-wide Sunday morning service to make a statement to our people and to the community that revival has come to our area and that we will never be the same again. One exciting prospect for the joint service: the united pastors will be the choir!

[The joint service was held at a convention center. Forty-seven hundred people showed up for an incredible time of praise and worship.]

As we pulled out in our vans from the conference center just after lunch time, we all realized that we had just experienced one of the greatest moments of our lives. God had truly visited sixty men. We were tired, but oh so grateful that the Lord in His wisdom had allowed these days together. They were certainly days of "heaven on earth." Now, to go home and see the fire spread!

As I've pondered the meaning of these precious days just past, a scene from the movie *Jesus of Nazareth* keeps coming to mind. Near the end of the film, one of the leaders of the Sanhedrin responsible for crucifying Jesus is sitting in his chamber. He has just learned that the body of Jesus is missing and that his followers are saying that He has risen from the dead. As he ponders the meaning of this turn of events, he thoughtfully mumbles to himself, as if perceiving the future consequences, "Now it *really* begins . . . now it *really* begins."

These are my sentiments at this hour. THE REVIVAL HAS BEGUN IN KITSAP COUNTY. Many have been saying for years that it was coming. Many things have been the prelude to this opening act. But now it is here. NOW IT REALLY BEGINS. And there will be no stopping it.

It is God's. He will do it. Each of us will either be a part of it through our obedience or we will watch it go by.

Lord, you know where my heart is! Bring on the rain!

From the Journal of Ron Boehme

Is a powerful movement of God possible in our generation? In your town and mine? In Kitsap County,

Washington? Across denominational and theological lines?

What is the greatest hindrance to the outpouring of God's Spirit? Dr. Paul Rees's observations serve as the beginning point for an answer. He writes:

> I shall go to my grave convinced that the Church—the visible community of Christian faith and fellowship—needs to exhibit a unity that is perilously contradicted by the exclusive, self-defensive, and often warring divisions into which we are fractured and fractioned ourselves. With time's passing, I am less impressed by our attempts to justify this rabbit-warren proliferating. I am increasingly struck by the flimsiness and self-serving of our arguments for going on as we are.

So why don't we change?

2

Satan blew out the lights of paradise.

The Eden conspiracy, birthed in hell, touched the very throne of heaven.

DIVISUS: It Started in the Garden

While the denizens of darkness rejoiced, Almighty God served his fallen creatures an eviction notice, a *divine divisus*, if you please. The party was over.

The book of Genesis reports that:

> After he drove the man out, he placed on the east side of the Garden of Eden cherubim and a flaming sword flashing back and forth to guard the way to the tree of life (Genesis 3:24).

Man—now a spiritually-gutted rebel, an accomplished fugitive from God, himself, and others—became a member of the kingdom of darkness, the *basileus satanas*.

Deeds of darkness followed.

Unity was replaced with disunity. Jealousy and competition overcame joy and encouragement. Strife snuffed out cooperative achievement. Self-centeredness diminished trust and loyalty. Divisions crippled human endeavors. Rival deities abounded. Relationships fell apart.

The Compromised Bride

From the fallen first couple to tomorrow's headlines, this satanically-inspired devastation continues. It comes as no surprise that spiritual warfare is one of Scripture's pervasive themes. In countless communities, the corporate power of networked churches has been neutralized and all but eliminated. The satanic seeds of discord have borne fruit.

At this point I should make it clear that I am not in any way downing the church and its valiant attempt to reach its world. For every troubled church there are some marvelous exceptions. Let me commend them and cast my vote for them. But my travels, observations, and conversations suggest that the church as a community of faith in a specific geographical area has little corporate impact, and in fact, has been neutralized.

I believe a Satanic stronghold, an unbiblical mindset, has the church in its grasp. Our Lord's prayer that believers would come to "complete unity" (John 17:23) is, for all practical purposes, viewed as divine rhetoric. More about this later.

Called to unity of the highest order, there is instead an ecclesiastical civil war raging between blood-bought brothers and sisters. Perhaps an "ecclesiastical standoff" would represent the actual state of many church fellowships. The battles have been fought, the lines have been drawn, the sheep have been carefully separated from the grunts—usually over externals that have little relevance to God's redemptive mission on this planet. Obviously, this civil war influences the attitudes and actions of the parishioner and his webs of relationships.

Someone has said that "the body and soul are so closely linked they catch each other's diseases." One might paraphrase it to say, "church leaders and parishioners are so closely linked they catch each other's diseases." If the leaders are "God's frozen people," church members will ice-skate down the aisles. Many feel that the greatest hindrance to revival is the pastor.

Both Paul and Christ address the importance of unity. The Corinthian church was a hotbed of disunity and turmoil. Paul did all he could to turn the situation around. With great concern he speaks against these life-sapping diseases.

> You are still worldly. For since there is jealousy and quarreling among you, are you not worldly? (1 Corinthians 3:3).

> I appeal to you, brothers . . . that all of you agree with one another so that there may be no divisions among you and that you may be perfectly united in mind and thought (1 Corinthians 1:10).

No divisions, perfectly united—surely you jest, Paul!

> Warn them before God against quarreling about words; it is of no value, and only ruins those who listen (2 Timothy 2:14).

No quarreling about etymological differences? What can we argue about?

> Make every effort to keep the unity of the Spirit through the bond of peace (Ephesians 4:3).

> Read the list again. It could be much longer, had I included all the references to you and me getting along.

How's Fishing?

Jesus put unity at the top of his prayer list. It's the theme of his high priestly prayer, the key to evangelistic effectiveness.

With a lost world on his mind,
with nails soon to pierce his hands and feet,
with ours sins about to be placed upon him,
with the welfare of the church weighing upon him,
with betrayal soon to take place,
Jesus prayed for unity.

Notice that the attainment and preservation of unity is a matter of divine enablement. John records Jesus' words:

Holy Father, protect them by the power of your name—the name you gave me—so that they may be one as we are one (John 17:11).

"Protect them . . . so that they may be one." Our Lord's request lead one to believe that there is someone at work attempting to thwart the unity of the Body of Christ. Experience confirms that suspicion.

Note carefully that the prerequisite for this unity is the new birth. Only those who by faith in Christ are members of the universal Church have the possibility of experiencing true unity.

I pray also for those who will believe in me . . .
that all of them may be one . . . (John 17:20,21).

Not some, not a few, not most, but *all.*

Furthermore, unity is not an option. He prays "that all of them may be one." All who are blood-bought, all who are genuine, born-again believers are to heed this call to unity. There are no exceptions.

Why not?

The maintenance of unity in a divided planet is central to God's redemptive purposes. It is the clear and decisive demonstration of that unity that attracts the lost to the cause of Christ.

The Acts 2 church is a model of this kind of unity.

They clung to the apostles' doctrine, they worshiped as one, they shared all they had and stood together against a pagan culture. Note Luke's description of the power of a united people:

> All the believers were one in heart and mind. No one claimed that any of his possessions was his own, but they shared everything they had (Acts 4:32).

> They broke bread in their homes and ate together with glad and sincere hearts, praising God and enjoying the favor of all the people (Acts 2:46-47).

Luke's account of this remarkable church closes with a glimpse of how God responds when true unity characterizes a church. "And the Lord added to their number daily those who were being saved" (2:47). Such people were uprooted from the kingdom of darkness and transplanted into the kingdom of light. Every single day!

The Achievement of Unity Is a Process

Jesus' request that we be brought to "complete unity" underscores that the realization of this unity is a process. It's not a quick-fix proposition. Nor is it likely to be negotiated around a council table. Wouldn't it behoove us to discover and encourage that process?

Our Lord's high-priestly prayer clearly teaches that unity is made in heaven, not on earth. That's where the ecumenical movement failed. Paul does not command the believers to make unity, but to keep and maintain the unity they have because they share the divine nature.

So what happened? Satan not only has blown out the lights of Paradise, he's declared war on the people of God throughout the ages. He opposes anything that encourages men and women to be united in Christ. Is it any wonder Satan turns man against God, woman against man, brother against brother, Cain against Abel, and church against church? And the broad path to eternal damnation remains packed with people.

Satan's Trump Card

If Satan considered the Eden Conspiracy his high-water mark, his *magnum opus*, what would you consider his second greatest coup?

Would splitting the kingdom of Israel be a candidate? If it's not number two on your list, you must admit it was a masterful stroke. When the kingdom divided, the unity, symmetry, and beauty of God lost its earthly incarnation. Three kings and it was all over: Saul, David, and Solomon.

What is said of Solomon helps us grasp the worldwide implications of Israel's mission.

> King Solomon was greater in riches and wisdom than all the other kings of the earth. The whole world sought audience with Solomon to hear the wisdom God had put in his heart (1 Kings 10:23-24).

The whole world sought audience with Solomon!

Israel wasn't intended to be some little nation stuck in a dark corner of the globe. She had a worldwide audience and a worldwide influence. Her calling was to be a witness to her world, to reveal to the nations what a God-flavored, divinely blessed, unified people looked like.

> You are my Servant, Israel, in whom I will display my splendor (Isaiah 49:3).

> I will also make you a light for the Gentiles, that you may bring my salvation to the ends of the earth (Isaiah 49:6).

Her mission was to make visible the invisible God so that the aliens in the land could discover and come to serve the only true God. For a while, the plan flourished.

At one time during Solomon's reign, "the people of Judah and Israel were as numerous as the sand on the seashore; they ate, they drank and they were happy" (1 Kings 4:20).

The Tale of Three Kings

Satan was actively at work long before the actual rupture of Solomon's kingdom. Note carefully that the first three kings did not escape the devil's web.

Consider the first king. Confronted by Goliath, King Saul punted. A young kid stepped in and saved Israel's hide. This young Goliath-buster became an instant national hero. Saul sulked. His growing jealousy got him in trouble again and again. In a fit of rage,

he killed eighty-five men who wore the linen ephod [priests]. He also put to the sword Nob, the town of the priests, with its men and women, its children and infants, and its cattle, donkeys and sheep (1 Samuel 22:18-19).

In over his head, he makes a beeline to the Witch of Endor hoping she could place a long-distance call to the late Samuel the prophet. He was seeking counsel from hell.

He finally committed suicide.

Following Saul's death, his military commander, Abner, immediately anointed Saul's son Ish-Bosheth as the new king of Israel. Samuel, however, had already been sent by God to anoint David as the next king. Civil war broke out between the houses of Saul and David. "The war between the house of Saul and the house of David," we are told, "lasted a long time" (2 Samuel 3:1). Ish-Bosheth's murder ended the tragic warfare. But Satan wasn't through with David.

The evil one was successful in getting David to act in deliberate disobedience to Yahweh, even though his general, Joab, warned him against it.

Satan rose up against Israel and incited David to take a census of Israel (1 Chronicles 21:1).

With great power the evil one arose and brought down in flames

- a giant-killer.
- a man after God's own heart.
- a godly leader.
- an informed administrator.
- a man completely aware of God's will on the matter.

A census was taken and seventy thousand Israelites died because of the king's disobedience.

And then there's Solomon. David's son, like so many biblical characters, failed in the second half of his life. The final chapter of Israel's leader is a sad one.

Solomon, the last king of the united kingdom, worshiped demonic spirits:

As Solomon grew old, his wives turned his heart after other gods. . . . He followed Ashtoreth the goddess of the Sidonians, and Molech the detestable god of the Ammonites (1 Kings 11:4-5).

Yahweh's king did what? He worshiped other gods? This was the same king, by the way, who built a fabulous temple to honor Yahweh, the only true God, the God who desired to incarnate himself in the lives of his people.

Two times in that sorry chapter we are told that God raised up adversaries against Solomon because of his apostasy. Satan drove a fatal wedge between God and his apostate king.

Saul, David, and Solomon were clearly influenced to plant the seeds of destruction in the nation they ruled. Ultimately, God said "Ichabod" to the whole thing.

The Laughingstock of the World

God planned to reveal himself through his people. His earthly address was P.O. Box 1, Jerusalem.

During its golden years, Israel had the attention and respect of the world. Though small, Jerusalem was a world-class city. In it God chose to dwell. It became his divine residence. And so it was for a while. But when the kingdom was torn apart, the divided people of God became a point of derision, the laughingstock of the world.

Ezekiel records God's description of the rise and fall of his chosen people. Note the verbs used to express God's efforts to prepare Israel for worldwide impact. It is an Old Testament equivalent of Christ nourishing and cherishing his Bride, the Church.

> I gave you my solemn oath and entered into a covenant with you, declares the Sovereign LORD, and you became mine.

> I bathed you with water and washed the blood from you and put ointments on you. I clothed you with an embroidered dress and put leather sandals on you. I dressed you in fine linen and covered you with costly garments.

I adorned you with jewelry: I put bracelets on your arms and a necklace around your neck, and I put a ring on your nose, earrings on your ears and a beautiful crown on your head.

So you were adorned with gold and silver; your clothes were of fine linen and costly fabric and embroidered cloth. Your food was fine flour, honey and olive oil.

You became very beautiful and rose to be a queen. And your fame spread among the nations on account of your beauty, because the splendor I had given you made your beauty perfect, declares the Sovereign LORD (Ezekiel 16:8-14).

Israel was gorgeous!

Obviously, the world didn't drop by the local bridal shop to admire her beauty. She wasn't some type of static display or a creature destined to show up at state fairs and ribbon-cutting ceremonies.

Such divinely bestowed beauty is always a reference to the beauty of character. It was God's splendor, the universals of His character, that was poured out upon Israel. The surrounding nations saw the very character of God made visible through the lives and actions of his people. They were "living epistles" to be read by all nations.

Please note it was God's initiative that rescued Israel from the rubbish heap, squirming in her blood. It was God who adorned her and put her on display. Beauty has always been the major component in the Father's evangelism strategy.

But Satan, then as now, does everything within his power to corrupt that beauty. Ezekiel reports how God's bride, the one through whom he displayed the universals of his character, became a two-bit whore:

> But you trusted in your beauty and used your fame
> to become a prostitute (Ezekiel 16:15).

From Bad to Worse

After the kingdom split, God's people turned inward and began fighting each other. Judah and Israel, sons of the covenant, became enemies. Ultimately, God withdrew his glory. Enmity reigned.

A civil war raged for generations. This war was not limited to throwing brickbats over a wall or attacking each other in theological journals. It was blood, sweat, and tears. It was a "hot war," not a cold one.

> There was continual warfare between Rehoboam
> [king of Judah] and Jeroboam [king of Israel]
> (2 Chronicles 12:15).

Jeroboam, wanting to keep Israel from returning to Jerusalem (part of Judah) to worship, set up rival temples complete with golden calves. The battles continued.

> There was war between Abijah [successor to
> Rehoboam] and Jeroboam. Abijah went into battle
> with a force of four hundred thousand able fighting
> men, and Jeroboam drew up a battle line against
> him with eight hundred thousand able troops
> (2 Chronicles 13:2-3).

Note again the number of soldiers.

> Abijah [king of Judah] and his men inflicted heavy
> losses on them, so that there were five hundred
> thousand casualties among Israel's able men
> (2 Chronicles 13:17).

Half a million folks slaughtered by their brothers. No

wonder the nations mocked! The calendar turns and the battle continues:

> So Jehoash king of Israel attacked. He and Amaziah king of Judah faced each other at Beth Shemesh in Judah. Judah was routed by Israel, and every man fled to his home (2 Chronicles 25:21-22).

> Jehoash king of Israel captured Amaziah king of Judah, the son of Joash, the son of Ahaziah, at Beth Shemesh. Then Jehoash brought him to Jerusalem and broke down the wall of Jerusalem from the Ephraim Gate to the Corner Gate—a section about six hundred feet long (2 Chronicles 25:23).

I probably should mention that not only did Jehoash rip down six hundred feet of the walls of the holy city, he pillaged the temple.

> He took all the gold and silver and all the articles found in the temple of God . . . together with the palace treasures and the hostages, and returned to Samaria (2 Chronicles 25:24).

We're talking about God's chosen people at war with God's chosen people. The sad saga continues:

> He [Ahaz, king of Judah] was also given into the hands of the king of Israel, who inflicted heavy casualties on him. In one day Pekah [king of Israel] . . . killed a hundred and twenty thousand soldiers in Judah (2 Chronicles 28:5-6).

In one day there were more casualties than the United States suffered in the Korean and Vietnam wars combined.

The children of the one true God have a tragic history

of civil war, whether hot or cold. It's likely Israel and Judah would have destroyed each other were it not for their continual warfare against the pagan kings of the land. Assyria eventually obliterated Israel, and Babylon destroyed Judah. The walls of Jerusalem were torn down and the gates burned. Jerusalem, the holy city, was in ruins. The banner of Yahweh was dragging in the dust.

Are We Any Different?

How sad, we think. But hasn't the same thing happened to the Church? The same God who rescued Israel from her filth and squalor also nourishes and cherishes his new-covenant Bride. He removes her spots and wrinkles so that she may incarnate the unity and beauty of God in her world. And yet listen to his indictment of the church in Thyatira:

> Nevertheless, I have this against you: You tolerate that woman Jezebel, who calls herself a prophetess. By her teaching she misleads my servants into sexual immorality . . . (Revelation 2:20).

I wish sexual immorality was confined to Thyatira, but it isn't. Sexual immorality is even now ravaging the church and its leaders.

No wonder that three times in our Lord's prayer for his church he asks his father to protect his blood-bought ones. The sad history of Israel certainly gave him reason to pray.

And not just about sexual immorality. He also knew of our propensity to war against each other. While we may not see dead bodies in the street, we're certainly not seeing lost "bodies" filling our pews. Eighty percent of the churches in the United States are not growing.

Each year the number of those attending our churches declines. Among the blood-bought, is it right that:

- non-charismatics denigrate the ministries of charismatics?
- mainline church members remain aloof from their brothers and sisters?
- independent churches look down on believers in mainline churches?
- churches are in competition with each other?
- ministers speak against their brothers and sisters?
- pastors have denominational blinders?
- church leaders sow seeds of discord between brothers?
- brothers exclude brothers from communion?
- those who will spend eternity together cannot get along here on earth?
- the non-believer has reason to scoff at Christianity because it is so divided?

I certainly would not suggest that all, or even the majority of churches are involved in internecine warfare. But benign neglect or rejection may be just as destructive.

Why doesn't someone call "time out"? Don't we understand what Paul said?

Stand firm in one spirit, contending as one man for the faith of the gospel (Philippians 1:27).

The Road Back

How do we respond to the ruins of our Jerusalems? Nehemiah's response is instructive. His model is convicting.

When I heard these things, I sat down and wept. For some days I mourned and fasted and prayed before the God of heaven.

Then I said, . . . "I confess the sins we Israelites, including myself and my father's house, have committed against you.

"Come, let us rebuild the wall of Jerusalem, and we will no longer be in disgrace" (Nehemiah 1:4-6; 2:17).

Note that Nehemiah put his finger on the real issue. God's reputation was disgraced, his character maligned by the collapsed walls and burned gates. The prophet Jeremiah surveyed the trashed city and, with a broken heart, wrote:

The roads to Zion [Jerusalem] mourn, for no one comes to her appointed feasts. All her gateways are desolate, her priests groan, her maidens grieve, and she is in bitter anguish (Lamentations 1:4).

All who pass your way clap their hands at you; they scoff and shake their heads at the Daughter of Jerusalem: "Is this the city that was called the perfection of beauty, the joy of the whole earth?" (Lamentations 2:15).

It was past tense. And couldn't something very similar be said of us today?

"Is this the Church, the spotless Bride of Christ, the perfection of beauty, the joy of the whole earth?"

It was . . . and could be again.

But where are our weeping prophets? Has the Church failed as Israel failed? Have we allowed a spirit of disunity and competition to blunt the effectiveness of the Body of Christ? Are we sowing discord among the brethren? Has unbelief limited the work of God in our midst?

Is genuine unity possible, or was the Lord's prayer heavenly rhetoric? Can ancient walls be rebuilt? Can the true body of Christ become one? Is "complete unity" possible?

Most rational people would say no. Why?

Could it be that a satanic stronghold exists right in the middle of the Church—a mindset that views as unchangeable that which clearly violates the expressed will of God?

Unity *is* the expressed, clearly stated will of God for his born-again children. Most of us in the evangelical community not only don't believe it will happen, we are suspicious of anyone attempting to promote it. Such rebel thoughts, not yet brought into captivity to Christ, are easy to discern.

"Unity? Won't see it in my lifetime."

"Unity is not and never has been a vital part of the church."

"Unity isn't possible. We're splintered into too many pieces."

"The call to unity is a plot of the Trilateral Commission."

"Unity is the door to liberalism."

"You can't have unity without compromise."

"Unity comes right out of the New Age Movement, or holistic medicine."

"Unity isn't part of the agenda for this dispensation."

"Joe Aldrich is a closet liberal."

But not everyone is caught up in such unbelief. Some are beginning to see Jesus' prayer in John 17 as something more than divine rhetoric. Listen to some

Christian leaders from diverse theological backgrounds who are beginning to experience what our Lord prayed about. God used a Prayer Summit to capture a few random thoughts:

> This has been an incredible four days for me. To be pressed to seek the Lord for our city with others of diverse temperament and theological views is very healthy and stretching.

> I believe this is the foundation for something great that Christ is going to do in Salem. The church has been divided too long. What a privilege to be part of something where the Body of Christ is brought together, where pastors can build trust toward each other and . . . see ourselves corporately as the church of Christ in Salem.

> *Pastor, Salem Alliance Church*

> To say it was answered prayer, the cry of God's heart, the cry of my heart for many years, would be an understatement in the extreme.

> If the pattern established by this conference is followed, if the momentum set in motion can be sustained, it cannot but be the beginning of true revival that quite likely will spread worldwide.

> *A Christian layman*

> I feel like I have been on a spiritual Mount of Transfiguration.

> *Pastor, Oak Park Church of God*

> We saw God build unity in diversity, love in strong dislike (hate). My heart was truly blessed.

> *Pastor, Robert Community Church*

Pastors representing a cross-section of denominations . . . gathered for prayer. God exceeded my expectation of the time.

Pastor, Salem Alliance Church

The spirit of oneness and unity among pastors of many different theological backgrounds . . . was a remarkable and supernatural phenomenon.

The renewed vision of our city of Salem's desperate need for spiritual revival and awakening was deeply impressed upon our broken hearts.

Pastor, Salem Lutheran Brethren

This week has been a wonderful spiritual adventure for me. God has met with me in revival. I met fellow pastors and feel closer to them than ever before. I believe that God has a plan for spiritual impact for our community. As He has bonded our hearts together, perhaps for the first time, he has the tools to put the plan into operation.

Pastor

To spend four days in prayer with my fellow ministers is not only refreshing, it builds a closeness I have never witnessed. What better way to combat a key tactic of Satan's plan but to unite the ministers?

Pastor, First Assembly of God

I came home with a new sense that I am not alone in the ministry, but am one with all the brothers who prayed together during those days.

Pastor, Boistfort Community Church

When you said "prayer conference," I don't believe I heard correctly. Or, maybe the name is a misnomer. We came to pray, but we beheld Jesus. I arrived as a pastor, I departed a believer. No amount of words could explain the depth, the warmth, the love, the mutual care that has been imparted as we've looked to the Lord of the Church. I eagerly anticipate the outworkings of this communion. And I wonder—how far will the Spirit of God breathe this life? Thank you for having no agenda but Christ.

Pastor

Thank you for the last four days at Cannon Beach. They have changed my life and my ministry. Before I came to this prayer conference I had thought of other churches as groups of people, buildings, and denominations. Now I see men, fellow pastors, with the same struggles, victories, joys, and hurts that I have. My relationships and my love for these men have grown deeply.

Pastor

Curious? I hope so. You might be encouraged to know that leaders from dozens of denominations are coming together around their love of Christ and concern for a lost world. The "divided kingdom" is being healed to the praise and glory of God.

It can be healed where you live, too.

3

THE DIVIDED KINGDOM: A Recovery Prototype

It hadn't happened in 250 years.

Could a twenty-five-year-old Judean king pull off a spiritual summit at Jerusalem? Would Israel accept an invitation to a united Passover Celebration, something which had not happened since the kingdom ruptured in the days of Solomon?

It was a daring dream planted by God in the heart of a newly crowned monarch named Hezekiah, the thirteenth king of Judah. The fact that his dad, King Ahaz, had offered several of his brothers as burnt sacrifices on a pagan altar undoubtedly influenced his decision.

During the reign of wicked Ahaz, the civil war between God's people continued. Disunity prevailed. Pekah led the armies of Israel against Jerusalem. In one day Pekah killed 120,000 people and took 200,000 captives. Ahaz, fearful for his life, pillaged the temple and shipped its riches to buy the support of Tiglath-Pileser king of Assyria. It wasn't a wise decision.

To appease Tiglath and perhaps tap his power, Ahaz replaced the altar in Jerusalem with an Assyrian one and offered sacrifices upon it to the gods of Damascus. He was playing theological roulette.

He shut the doors of the LORD's temple and set up altars at every street corner in Jerusalem. In every town in Judah he built high places to burn sacrifices to other gods . . . (2 Chronicles 28:24-25).

They also shut the doors of the portico and put out the lamps (2 Chronicles 29:7).

Ahaz was a wicked, conniving, compromising weakling who'd sell his soul to attain his ends. Imagine growing up in that household! His own son said, "Enough is enough."

The Beginnings of Revival

In the first month of his reign, Hezekiah opened the doors of the temple of the Lord. No doubt it needed airing out.

It should not surprise us that God directed Hezekiah to begin the revival by consecrating the priests. These religious leaders had failed to maintain their own hearts and had neglected the disciplines of their faith and service. God's first priority was to cleanse his house and its leadership.

The temple itself was unclean, and thus nonfunctional. Oh, it had a heated baptistry, a modern nursery, a mammoth pipe organ, and a grand piano . . .

They brought out to the courtyard of the LORD's temple everything unclean that they found in the temple of the LORD. The Levites took it and carried it out to the Kidron Valley (2 Chronicles 29:16).

Hezekiah's generation cleaned house, hauling off all that was unholy.

In the process of cleaning the temple, all that was

unholy was publicly exposed. It probably was good that the priests and Levites actually had to lift and haul the garbage. They had to touch it, to rub their noses in it. Undoubtedly it weighed heavily upon them. And that's not all bad. Wouldn't you suspect that with hands full of abomination, their hearts would be full of repentance?

God is to be worshiped in the beauty of holiness. Hezekiah had no other agenda. His goal wasn't even to "win" the nation. He felt burdened to restore the true worship of God. So worshiped, God will draw men unto himself, and to each other.

So they carted away all that was an abomination to the God of holiness. They took the trash to the trash heap. Imagine the emotion of it. They got rid of all that would hinder fellowship and worship. It took them sixteen days to get rid of the junk and prepare themselves and their neglected temple for worship.

Mark it well, friend: What they did took courage. The local folks had worshiped at these pagan altars for generations. I'm sure they didn't all respond positively to the destruction of their altars. But they had no say in the matter. Their favorite shrine simply disappeared. Period.

The next order of business was the sin offering. And sinned they had. They made no excuses. Humbled, they confessed:

> Our fathers were unfaithful; they did evil in the eyes of the LORD our God and forsook him. They turned their faces away from the LORD's dwelling place and turned their backs on him (2 Chronicles 29:6).

Don't let the fact that they confessed the sins of their fathers slip by. They must be confessed if God is going to release his blessing.

Notice that Hezekiah commanded that the sin offering be made for all Israel, not just Judah.

> The priests then slaughtered the goats and presented their blood on the altar for a sin offering to atone for all Israel, because the king had ordered the burnt offering and the sin offering for all Israel (2 Chronicles 29:24).

The king already visualizes a kingdom reunited around the Passover Feast. Wasn't it the theological core that Israel and Judah shared in common? It's interesting, isn't it, that this young king prays for God's favor upon his enemies, the ones who killed 120,000 of his people while his dad served as king?

He didn't seek revenge, he sought restoration. He wasn't exclusive, he was inclusive. He desired the benefits of forgiveness to accrue to his enemies.

His home base now in order, he sent out invitations to the party. The invitation read, "come as you are." Couriers were sent throughout Israel and Judah, from "Dan to Beersheba." This Pony Express headed to all points of the compass. They bore messages calling the people to come to Jerusalem and celebrate the Passover to the Lord. Wrapped up in the trip was a basic assumption: repentance, renunciation, and reconciliation.

The letter was a call to abandon their unfaithfulness, cease being "stiff-necked," and submit to the Lord. Previous generations fell to the surrounding nations because their leaders failed to bring their people to repentance. It was a serious invitation. God would not sanction their fallen state with his power—and with war-clouds gathering, they needed God to act on their behalf.

The People's Response

As you can well imagine, the invitation received mixed reviews.

> The couriers went from town to town . . . but the people scorned and ridiculed them (2 Chronicles 30:10).

So what's new? After all, wasn't the idea of a divided kingdom returning to its spiritual roots a preposterous scheme? It hadn't happened in over two hundred years. Furthermore, it would violate all the other religious communities that had captured the loyalty of the chosen people. Idolatry was everywhere. Wouldn't rival priesthoods be concerned about this return to Jerusalem?

Besides, the bad blood had existed for generations. Civil wars are ugly and hard to forget. They fuel revenge, not repentance. The ramifications of countless casualties, not to mention a six hundred-foot patch in the wall of Jerusalem, are not easily forgotten. For uncounted years they had hated each other. Furthermore, it's fun to be bitter—in a perverse sort of way.

But thank God for the remnant of faith. Those who saw beyond the rubbish, the burned gates, and the destroyed relationships. Those whose hearts longed for unity. Those who understood the evangelistic implications of a lifestyle of unity. Those who longed for reunion.

> Nevertheless, some men . . . humbled themselves and went to Jerusalem (2 Chronicles 30:11).

Nevertheless means "in spite of." In spite of the ridicule and scorn, some were big enough to sense the rightness of heeding the call to unity. Undoubtedly they hoped such a spiritual summit could bring healing and restoration to a horribly divided religious community. Perhaps they perceived the benefit that would accrue to the marriages, families, and communities of those who made the pilgrimage. In church growth circles, it's called "redemptive lift."

It is significant that Hezekiah's vision was not a call to a lectureship or a conference on unity. He could have asked the Prophets Isaiah or Micah to speak on the subject. The problem, however, wasn't intellectual. Nothing less than a prolonged meeting with God in repentance, reconciliation, and worship had much chance of tearing down the walls of mistrust and hate.

Hezekiah's invitation was a return to the basics, a call to celebrate an ancient deliverance memorialized by the Passover Feast. It was a call to return to their roots, to come together around that which unites, to focus on their common deliverance from four hundred years of slavery. It was a chance to raise Yahweh's banner out of the dust.

Hezekiah's Solemn Assembly was really nothing radical. God's original plan for his people was that they would come together in Jerusalem three times each year!

This "Solemn Assembly" was to be a time for doing business with God. The ancient city of David was the theological center of the world, the place where God put his name, where he met with his people. Their systematic "coming togethers" were designed to send them back to their towns and villages united again around Yahweh and his plans for them. If carefully adhered to, a continuous renewal of faith and commitment was virtually assured.

Revival was built into the calendar of those twelve

special tribes. This pattern had to be corrupted, had to be broken if Israel's revelatory mission was to be aborted. And so it was. Yes, "Satan rose up against Israel."

And then along came Hezekiah with an impossible dream.

Those who chose to return to Jerusalem are said to have "humbled themselves." They had to swallow their pride, go against public opinion, and perhaps face the ridicule of their peers. Undoubtedly part of their humiliation was an admission of their sin and their need to confess it and seek reconciliation.

Certainly the king's proclamation stirred up debate in virtually every town and village to which the couriers delivered their challenging invitation.

"Don't trust a twenty-five-year-old. He's just a kid. He'll get over it."

"His motives. It's his motives that are wrong."

"Are you kidding? Go to Jerusalem? We've got plenty of temples right here in town."

"It's another plot to steal our sheep."

"We'll be compromising if we join with them in worship."

"Hezekiah's a charismatic. You can't trust those charismatics."

"We've been fighting for two hundred years, why should we stop now?"

Thank God for the exceptions. For those who did humble themselves. Certainly such "isolationism" isn't God's will for them. It wasn't then, and it isn't now.

The Origin of the Plan

I'm excited to report that this whole escapade was not the dream of a wild-eyed visionary. It was God's idea.

Also in Judah the hand of God was on the people to give them unity of mind to carry out what the king and his officials had ordered, following the word of the LORD (2 Chronicles 30:12).

"Following the word of the LORD." The king simply implemented God's vision.

Despite those who scorned and ridiculed, "a very large crowd of people assembled in Jerusalem to celebrate the Feast of Unleavened Bread in the second month" (30:13). As far as we know, they left their weapons home. That in itself was a step of faith. What a glorious scene it must have been!

Once they arrived, these pilgrims pitched in and helped the locals prepare the rest of the city for the party.

Restoring the long-neglected temple had proven to be a herculean task for the locals. No problem. The first thing the out-of-town folks did was roll up their sleeves and rid the city of Jerusalem of its pagan altars. They dumped them in the Kidron Valley—just piled them on top of all the garbage hauled out of the desecrated temple. All rivals to the one true God were thrown out.

When this happens, reunion is right around the corner.

Theological compatibility was the foundation of this remarkable spiritual house-cleaning. Revival tarries until the shrines are torn down and heresy is exposed and disposed of. Not a theologically neutral reunion, its participants rallied around the ancient truth of the Passover Feast. Such theological and conceptual unity is foundational to other more visible expressions of unity.

This was a hastily called summit. Priests and common folks came to the feast spiritually unprepared. It was logistically impossible for them to meet the Levitical requirements for participation in the Passover. Yet sacrifices were offered anyway. By unconsecrated priests, for unconsecrated people.

Alarmed, Hezekiah sought the Lord. Because our Lord recognized their sincerity, he allowed these unconsecrated priests to offer sacrifices for unconsecrated people. He's always been responsive to seeking hearts. The text says,

> The Israelites who were present in Jerusalem celebrated the Feast of Unleavened Bread for seven days with great rejoicing, while the Levites and priests sang to the LORD every day, accompanied by the LORD's instruments of praise (2 Chronicles 30:21).

They came back for seconds. Can you imagine? Church folks normally start shaking their watches if the preacher goes a minute or two beyond "closing time." By and large, the church has lost the dynamics of corporate gatherings. Not Israel!

> The whole assembly then agreed to celebrate the festival seven more days; so for another seven days they celebrated joyfully (30:23).

Can you believe it? They signed on for another seven days of glorious worship and celebration. How excited Hezekiah must have been!

> The entire assembly of Judah rejoiced . . . and all who had assembled from Israel, including the aliens who had come from Israel . . . (30:25).

Don't miss the aliens. Praise God! They joined the party.

> There was great joy in Jerusalem, for since the days of Solomon . . . there had been nothing like this in Jerusalem. The priests and the Levites

stood to bless the people, and God heard them, for their prayer reached heaven, his holy dwelling place (2 Chronicles 30:26-27).

United, broken, crushed, healed, and reunited in worship, they became one. It no longer mattered whether they were from Israel or Judah, God's chosen ones or aliens, poor or rich, bond or free. Tribal affiliation was unimportant. They had met with God in a profound way. Their parched souls were restored, their empty hearts were filled, their sins were forgiven, their unity was recovered.

All had been humbled.

All had been blessed.

All had been restored.

Lectures wouldn't have produced this unity. It was birthed from two weeks of worshiping God—something nearly impossible to experience in our church services or speaker-centered retreats. Their experience of God was so profound, their joy so complete, they had to have another week of worship. And so they did. Read carefully and meditate upon the results:

> When all this had ended, the Israelites who were there went out to the towns of Judah, smashed the sacred stones and cut down the Asherah poles. They destroyed the high places and altars throughout Judah and Benjamin and in Ephraim and Manasseh. After they had destroyed all of them, the Israelites returned to their own towns and to their own property (2 Chronicles 31:1).

It was a demolition derby of cosmic proportions.

Their generation experienced revival. With a Spirit-born militancy, they went out and boldly confronted the

fortress of hell and filled up many "Kidron Valleys" with
the ruins of the idols they smashed and the altars they
destroyed. After they neutralized all of them, they went
home. And what a homecoming it must have been!
Their lamps flickered into the wee hours of the morning
as the pilgrims shared their joy.

And the heaps!

Have you ever heard of Hezekiah's heaps? Following
the great prayer summit, Hezekiah saw to it that the
financial needs of running the temple were provided for.
He reminded his people that they were to bring offerings
to underwrite the temple services so that the priests and
Levites "could devote themselves to the law of God."
Then one day he was walking outside and saw the heaps.

> Hezekiah asked the priests . . . about the heaps;
> and Azariah the chief priest . . . answered, "Since
> the people began to bring their contributions to
> the temple of the LORD, we have had enough to
> eat and plenty to spare, because the Lord has
> blessed his people, and this great amount is left
> over" (2 Chronicles 31:9-10).

There was great joy in Jerusalem. Mark it well.
Revival not only unleashes the power of God, it touches
the pocketbooks of men.

> So the service of the temple . . . was reestablished.
> Hezekiah and all the people rejoiced at what God
> had brought about for his people, *because it was done
> so quickly* (2 Chronicles 29:35-36, emphasis mine).

They didn't even have time to buy TV spots or place
ads in the *Jerusalem Post*. It happened without CNN or
ABC.

The Impossible Dream

God planted a dream in the heart of a rookie king from a wicked background. It was a dream about unity, a dream about repentance, reconciliation and restoration. Strongholds were raised against it. The idea was ridiculed and scorned. It was tested.

But it happened. And for a brief time in the dark history of Israel, one generation experienced a taste of what God desired all along: that they be one. Those who humbled themselves and came to the party went away on fire for their God.

They still do.

Do you believe God would be pleased to move in a mighty way among his people today? Is it possible they could be called back to unity and end the civil war that is so disruptive to the cause of Christ? Can we see the day when God is pleased to "add daily to their number those who are being saved?" Could a renewed church displace the forces of darkness which rule our cities? It would take a miracle. But then, our God is good at miracles.

An Ancient King's Steps to Reunitus

Let's close this chapter by reviewing Hezekiah's plan for *reunitus* and seeing whether we might not find wisdom in his plan. The Lord knows we could use some!

1. The king's theological convictions inspired him to take a bold and risky chance.

This isn't a bad place for renewal and revival to begin. Somebody's got to step into the spiritual vacuum and "swing, hot or cold." God withholds revival fires if leadership lacks vision, faith, humility, and courage.

Pastor, what are you doing to bring about true unity in your community? Church leader, are you part of the problem or part of the answer? You say no one in your area has such a vision? Then why don't you be the first to "get it"? It has to start somewhere. Why not with you?

2. The revival began with genuine repentance on the part of Israel's leaders.

In the same manner, contemporary *reunitus* begins with humbled and broken pastors who take holiness seriously. The priests and Levites, we are told, "were ashamed" (2 Chronicles 30:15).

As Francis Frangipane says, "Before God moves in power, it seems, he moves in holiness." Pastoral Prayer Summits often result in humility, brokenness, and shame. It is the first step toward renewal.

3. The refuse and garbage of the past was thrown out of the temple.

In like manner, churches full of rancor, strife, and division are filled with unclean things that need to be jettisoned.

I can't help but wonder how many junk-filled dumpsters would be on their way to the sanitary landfill if the Church cleaned house of all that is a disgrace to the Lord of the Church. Things like ecclesiastical kingdom building, competition, lack of vision, compromise, and theological drift. I suppose I'd be curious to see what was in that proverbial dumpster. Let's leave it at this: You fill your truck, and I'll fill mine.

On the positive side, what could we toss out if God's agenda were the only one that mattered? I think we'd be amazed at what we could get along without.

R. A. Torrey says the first step toward revival is for a group of people to get themselves thoroughly right with God. Dare we approach the temple mount without first carrying the idols of our lives to the Kidron Valley dump? Is it possible that most of the idols are more than one man can bear? Could it be that genuine healing comes when we invite others to help us bear our faults to the valley? Now that could be threatening . . . and life-changing.

4. *The true people of God, from all parts of the nation, strangled their pride and gathered for corporate praise and confession.*

By and large, the church has forgotten that there is great power in corporate gatherings. We have neglected the evangelistic impact of such events.

Funny how pride keeps us from coming together around that which is substantial and essential. Tragic, isn't it, that denominational or theological pride often precludes believers from participating in God's call to maintain unity in spite of our diversity?

"Me? Meet with Presbyterians? You're out of your mind."

"We Baptists have a long tradition of separatism, and this ploy isn't about to change that now."

"Hell will freeze over before I'll worship with a dispensationalist."

"We've got a large and influential congregation. We can't come to the party."

Thank God for those who do humble themselves and come to the party. There's no other way to attract the blessing of God. It's my observation that the ancient sin of pride is the major reason pastors minister in isolation from others of like, precious faith.

Having now participated in dozens of prayer summits, I've observed it takes at least two days of worship and prayer before conviction impels believers to initiate their own pilgrimage to the Kidron Valley.

The trip to the "Valley of Shame" is a perilous journey because it often necessitates the tearing down of the stronghold of pride. Yet there is no healing without humility. It's never easy to "come clean" before God and your peers. Perhaps even more challenging is the setting aside of the pastoral role to become a vulnerable, authentic pilgrim. Revival demands nothing less than cleansed and reconsecrated leadership.

Mark it well: Humility is the first step toward unity. Without it, unity is a pipe dream.

Twentieth-century leaders should be curious about what captures the attention of God and releases divine enablement. God does not release spiritual power and enablement indiscriminately.

Unfortunately, too few spiritual tour guides schedule the trip to the Kidron Valley. All rival claims on our time, energy, and resources deserve only the rubbish heap. When God's invitation comes, we have but two options: laugh and scorn, or humble ourselves, detour to the valley, and approach the holy mount—together.

5. *The corporate gathering at Jerusalem precipitated an unprecedented outpouring of God's blessing.*

How often an honest pilgrimage to the Kidron Valley begins the flow of divine healing and restoration! Here's the principle: Great healing is followed by great revival.

It's astonishing how four or five days of prayer and worship make denominational labels seem so insignificant. And it's phenomenal how the Lord uses this new found unity to radically transform the spiritual landscapes of once-barren communities.

Lord, Bring It On!

Is the kind of victory experienced by Israel under Hezekiah possible today? Thank God, the answer is yes!

Hundreds of pastors throughout the Pacific Northwest are discovering that, not only is it possible, it's mandatory. If the church is to become what Jesus prayed for in John 17, it must happen.

Prayer Summits have a way of nudging folks toward that goal. Blood-bought brothers who once were at odds with each other have come together as one and are beginning to see remarkable fruit in orchards that formerly grew only thistles and weeds. These believers have discovered the divine power of unity.

But what exactly is this stuff called unity? What does it look like? And how do you get it? That's what we'll look into next.

4

ONE + ONE = ONE: Permanently Stuck with Each Other

Lazarus, come forth!"

He did.

As Lazarus waltzed away hand-in-hand with Mary and Martha, the war escalated. The stool pigeons in the crowd flapped their way to the Pharisees and sang like songbirds. A meeting was called. Ruffled feathers led to some off-the-record decisions that sealed the fate of this itinerant preacher. Or so they thought.

The decision of the Sanhedrin made sense. "What are we accomplishing?" they asked. Not much. Very little, in fact. These religious leaders had nothing in their bag of tricks to equal a resurrection. Embarrassed, thoroughly upstaged, unable to up the ante, they voted to eliminate him.

If we let him go on like this, everyone will believe in him, and then the Romans will come and take away both our place [temple] and our nation (John 11:48).

Caiaphas, the high priest, listened for awhile and then chided them for their ignorance. Rome wasn't the issue. Jesus, he suggested, was not only going to die for the Jewish nation, but for all the scattered children of God "to bring them together and make them one" (John 11:52).

Wouldn't that be awful!

Caiaphas was right. Jesus intended to bring Jews and Gentiles together and make them one. Is it any wonder that from that day they plotted to take his life?

Caiaphas's charges weren't based on idle speculation. Hadn't Jesus just lectured on true and false shepherds and proclaimed that he was the only true one? He had other sheep, he said, "that are not of this sheep pen. I must bring them also. They too will listen to my voice, and there shall be one flock and one shepherd" (John 10:16).

Those were fighting words.

If Jesus could pull it off, they'd be unemployed. Eventually they crucified him and thought it was done with. It wasn't. The very death they orchestrated provided the basis for the unity the true Shepherd talked about. "His purpose," Paul wrote, "was to create in himself one new man out of the two, thus making peace, and in this one body to reconcile both of them to God through the cross, by which he put to death their hostility" (Ephesians 2:15-16).

"Through the cross." How ironic. Caiaphas and his cohorts saw to it that Jesus died, and that very death killed the hostility that kept Jew and Gentile from being one.

In heavenly math, one + one = one. When a butcher cleaves, he makes two out of one. When a husband cleaves, he makes one out of two. In the Church, all become one. Galatians 3:28 tells us that "there is neither Jew nor Greek, slave nor free, male nor female, for you are all one in Christ Jesus." All we need to do is act like we're "all one."

What Does It Mean to Be One?

Let's be clear about what we mean when we talk about "being one."

If it's the goal of unity to get folks to stop feuding, hold hands, and pump sunshine, count me out. I've never been into the warm fuzzies scene. While unity has overtones of peace and tranquility, it's a war word, birthed in battle. We're coached to be one, to stand together in the midst of the onslaught.

Like Nehemiah.

His sword and shovel defense strategy is worth emulating. A trumpet blast down the wall meant the enemy had launched an attack and the comrades needed help.

Preferences aside, when the trumpet sounds, God expects his children to come to the aid of their brothers and sisters regardless of their labels. That's unity.

Unity is a noun. That means it's either a person, place, or thing. A quick process of elimination tells us unity is a thing. It's something that can be observed and experienced. It wins football games. The United States Olympic hockey team had it when they defeated the mighty Soviets in 1980 and took home the gold medal. The rag-tag American kids were one in heart, soul, and spirit. They put it all on the line and won. They couldn't be denied. Their unity allowed them to play beyond their ability.

So what is this "oneness" that Jesus and others think is so important? Two Greek words will help us see its significance. Perhaps the famous feud between the Hatfields and McCoys will illustrate these two usages. If you attack one Hatfield, you've attacked them all. They're blood brothers, they're kinfolk, they're organically related because Hatfield blood runs through their veins. They'll stand together until the last man because of this organic relationship. Blood is thicker than water.

Kinship aside, they're also one in their desire to

eliminate the McCoys. They act in unity, not simply
because they're next of kin, but because they share a
common goal. Theoretically, the Hatfields and
McCoys might find themselves cooperating if they
shared a common hatred of another group (like the
Feds). As you may have guessed, the first Greek word
speaks of organic relatedness; the second, of issue-
relatedness.

The first term, the most common Greek word for
"one" [heis], is rarely used as a digit, like "she bought one
potato." It often refers to that which is one-of-a-kind, or
unique. Sometimes it refers to that which is unanimous
because people are of "one" heart. When such a group of
people is perceived as "one," this "oneness" suggests an
organic unity growing out of family or ethnic relationships.

The feuding Hatfields and McCoys had this organic
unity. You hit one and you've hit them all. You offend
one and the whole pack is at your doorstep. You're in
trouble! Regardless of their own quarrels, they were of
"one accord" when the clan came under attack.

But the Hatfields were not only one because Hatfield
blood flowed through their veins, they were also one in
their desire to eliminate the McCoys. Family ties and a
common cause glued them together.

The second term for unity [homothudomon] describes
people who are united around a common cause.

So what is unity? Greek usage suggests that it is both
a cooperative behavior that stems from relationship and
a shared mission. The second New Testament term
highlights the task or mission dimensions of unity.
People act in unity because they are of one mind on a
specific issue or cause. Unanimity in this case is issue
driven, not organically driven.

Unity in the New Testament

The following usages underscore a unity or oneness that grows out of agreement about a specific mission or cause.

When the day of Pentecost came, they were all together in one place (Acts 2:1).

When they heard this, they raised their voices together in prayer to God (Acts. 4:24).

It seemed good to us, having become of one mind (Acts 15:25, NASB).

People who may have fought like cats and dogs, "ran upon him [Stephen] with one accord" (Acts 7:57, KJV). At the riot in Ephesus, they "rushed as one man into the theater," (Acts 19:29).

This "one mindedness" is not the expression of a settled religious disposition or organic connectedness. Rather, it speaks of a group's response to an external event or threat. While New Testament usage of this term does stress the inner unanimity of the community, the roots of that unanimity are external. And there's nothing wrong with that! If a Democrat's house is burning down, it is praiseworthy if a political adversary, a Republican, mans a hose in common cause. Once the fire's out, they can resume slinging mud. A burning house supersedes the lack of organic unity between political opponents.

Although the members of Nehemiah's construction crew were one in heart and mind, they were about as diverse a bunch as you'll ever find. For sure they weren't a bunch of hard hats from the local union hall. They were:

priests
nobles
goldsmiths

perfume-makers
rulers
women
Levites
servants
merchants

Eighteen-wheelers worked next to jewelers, catskinners rubbed shoulders with accountants and CPA's. Masons worked hand-in-hand with perfume merchants.

The rough and the calloused passed bricks to women. The coarse and the refined were co-laborers. Some talked about investments. Other conversations centered around 4x4's and the hottest fishing holes. A few may have discussed philosophy and religious issues. One thing they shared in common: a deep commitment to rebuild the disgraced city of God and reestablish the fear of the Lord. And what was the result?

As the walls went up and the new gates were hung, fear descended upon the enemies of those who dared to rebuild the ruins.

A clear vision cuts a mighty path through obstacles. When the members of the broader community of faith join hands in the task of magnifying Almighty God and seeking His agenda together, they are able to transcend their often self-centered agendas and personal tensions. Walls come down when we join together in the worship and service of Yahweh-God. Furthermore, unity strikes fear in the heart of the enemy.

What Does Unity Accomplish?

Those who came to Hezekiah's Solemn Assembly saw what united praise and worship could do. But that was centuries ago. Could something like it happen in our generation?

Words simply cannot express my heartfelt thanks to God for the four days we had at Cannon Beach! I'll never be the same again. I can never look at Lewis County the same again. I can only "see" the bigger picture of the body of Christ scattered throughout Centralia, Chehalis, Morton, Winlock, Toledo, Boistfort, Randle, Packwood, Vader, Doty, Pe Ell, Napavine, Onalaska, Mossyrock, Adna, etc., where the Lord has his warriors laboring for his kingdom and loving and worshipping the same Lord who brought us redemption!

Pastor

Mossyrock? Vader? You've never heard of them. The Morton church averages about a dozen folks each Sunday. Yet this group of rural pastors decided to have a joint service to declare their oneness.

Twenty-five hundred people showed up at the local high school for this unique event. About two dozen pastors became the choir and sang their hearts out to the Lord as they stood arm-in-arm before the crowd. There were lots of tears!

Events like this demonstrate that unity can be both internally and externally motivated. People unite for both organic and task reasons. They get along because they belong to each other and because they are united in common cause.

Unity is a miracle. If the church of Christ stood together as a harmonious community of brothers and sisters where love and peace ruled, it would be such a unique phenomenon in our egotistical culture that everyone would be forced to acknowledge that it is divine in its origin.

Unity is a victory. All unity has a perceived outcome

that somehow overcomes the gravitational pull toward
disunity. We see it in athletics, in battle, and in business. If the cause is grand enough and rewarding
enough, thieves will unite in common cause.
Unfortunately, much of so-called "unity" centers around
personal gain at the expense of others. It's called greed.
When "Thy kingdom come" becomes "my kingdom
come," the blessing of God goes somewhere else.

The Foundation of Christian Unity

There are two essential "joinings" that constitute the
foundation for Christian unity. Without these two joinings, it is doubtful believers would ever come together in
common cause. Because of these two joinings, they have
no option. That is, they have no option if they want to
please Him.

Through the New Birth you are supernaturally joined
to Christ. This is the first joining. Jesus used some
organic metaphors to describe this reality:

He is the vine, we are the branches.
He is the groom, we are the bride.
He is the head, we are the body.

The night of his betrayal, Jesus talked about this joining with his disciples. "On that day," he told them, "you
will realize that I am in my Father, and you are in me,
and I am in you" (John 14:20). Sounds like we are all
tossed into a divine blender of some sort! "You are in
me" he said. Every believer is "in Christ." The implications are significant:

Therefore, if anyone is in Christ, he is a new cre-
ation; the old has gone, the new has come!"
(2 Corinthians 5:17).

The new comes when this union bears fruit, when the branches draw sustenance from the vine, when the body responds to its head.

A Presbyterian believer and a Baptist believer are joined to the same vine, they're engaged to the same Lord, they're in the same sheepfold, they're stones in the same building, they're indwelt by the same Spirit. They probably even study the same Book and sing the same hymns. Isn't that adequate reason to get along? The imagery is not of one tree trunk (vine) nourishing just one branch. The life of God flows to myriads of branches. God has no "only child."

There's a second joining. The first is vertical between man and God. The second is horizontal between man and man. Through the baptism of the Spirit, all believers are joined to the Body of Christ. That is, we are sovereignly placed into the Universal Church composed of all who through faith have received Christ as their savior.

For we were all baptized by one Spirit into one body—whether Jews or Greeks, slave or free— and we were all given the one Spirit to drink (1 Corinthians 12:13).

One body, one Spirit. It's believers united to Christ and each other whom God is calling to unity—those who name the name of Christ in the different communities of faith.

Paul reminds us in 1 Corinthians 12:27 that "now you are the body of Christ, and each one of you is a part of it." "Each member," he reminds the Roman church, "belongs to all the others" (Romans 12:5). Paul seems to anticipate that some folks are going to want to check out of this body. He slams the door on that option.

Some want out because they're different and proud of

it. "If the foot should say, 'Because I am not a hand, I do not belong to the body,' it would not for that reason cease to be part of the body" (1 Corinthians 12:15). The Presbyterians have no basis for feeling superior to the Independent Bible Church.

Slam!

Others want out because they don't need anyone else. Paul's answer? "The eye cannot say to the hand, 'I don't need you!'" (1 Corinthians 12:21). The Baptist can't say to the Charismatic "I don't need you."

Slam!

Like it or not, we're "members of one another." Furthermore, we're interdependent. We need each other. And the world needs us to be biblical in our support and concern for each other. God's desire is that "there should be no division in the body, but that its parts (that's all of us) should have equal concern for each other. If one part suffers, every part suffers with it; if one part is honored, every part rejoices with it" (1 Corinthians 12:25-26). We're to rejoice and suffer together!

Paul's letter to the Ephesians reminds us that the body (all believers of every color, stripe, and flavor) mutually edifies and "builds itself up in love, as each part does its work" (Ephesians 4:16). We need some proper working!

Please note that these joinings:
- are divine in their origin.
- are permanent in their duration.
- transcend denominational loyalties and all human institutions.
- cannot be altered by Satan. He can attack the fruit (unity), but not the root (our union with Christ and each other).
- are the basis for unity.

Does unity mean we always have to agree or be the same? Absolutely not! In 1991 President Bush instructed Sadaam Hussein that in the United States there is diversity, but not division.

Unity is not unanimity. Nor is it uniformity. When there is a lot of pressure for uniformity, we don't have unity. When we have true unity, we don't all have to be the same. Furthermore, unity is not union. God has not called us into some kind of structural or organizational union. Paul's command is that we keep (not make) the unity that we already have because of our union with Christ.

Is Unity Really Possible?

Unity sounds great, but is it possible? Can it work? Has it ever worked? Listen to Dr. Luke's diagnosis:

> All the believers were one in heart and mind. No one claimed that any of his possessions was his own, but they shared everything they had. With great power the apostles continued to testify to the resurrection of the Lord Jesus, and much grace was upon them all. There were no needy persons among them. For from time to time those who owned lands or houses sold them, brought the money from the sales and put it at the apostles' feet, and it was distributed to anyone as he had need (Acts 4:32-35).

Just imagine! There were no divisions among them. They were not dominated by material possessions. They were generous with all they had. They addressed human need in a powerful and sacrificial manner. They experienced daily conversions (Acts 2). They found favor with all the people (Acts 2).

If I join Rotary and you join Rotary, we're Rotarians! Even though you drive a Ford and I prefer Chevrolets. If we're both joined to Christ through the New Birth, we're both Christians, even if you prefer the King James Bible and I use the NIV. Like it or not, we're brothers and sisters—forever. Furthermore, the Spirit's baptism, like a giant blender, joined us to one another in an indissoluble union. We're now "members of one another." Because we're organically linked in permanent union, the Lord prayed we'd be his players, effectively reflecting the unity of the blessed trinity.

If I'm joined to Christ and you're joined to Christ, we're joined to each other.

Permanently.

5

UNITED WE STAND: The John 17 Connection

God was there. His presence was so real that for twenty or more minutes not a pastor said a word. Many were weeping silently. Some were flat on their faces on the carpet.

For three days they had sought the Lord. Hour after hour they'd been in his presence, seeking his agenda for their lives and ministries. Walls had come down. Three days of worship, confession, and repentance had brought them to this sacred time of silence. Souls were so full they couldn't take any more. No one dared to speak.

It was, I believe, a holy hush.

One by one they approached the communion table. Most wept as they served themselves the elements and then returned quietly to their seats. Their minds were still trying to process the events of the preceding days.

Many wondered how they had missed it for so long. John 17 was becoming a reality for them. Though most had passed tests in the theology of the Church, few had personally experienced the reality of the church as a responding family and a healing communion. Used to being agents of the liberating power of the gospel, they found themselves the objects of it. Used to ministering, they found themselves the object of ministry at a deep and significant level. Used to talking about God, they listened to God talking to them.

Once they sensed heaven was open, pastors found themselves sitting in that "hated chair" pouring out their hearts to God as their new-found friends listened and ministered to them. Dozens of times those who spoke were surrounded by brothers who laid their hands on them and entered into their pain. Strangely absent were prayers for:

Aunt Matilda's arthritic hip.

missionaries.

church activities.

denominational concerns.

the downtrodden.

Important as these requests may be, God clearly had a different agenda. So what did they share? Some confessed their spiritual bankruptcy. Others acknowledged their doubts and fears. Many admitted besetting sins. Others spoke of their need to be delivered from the memory and pain of abusive backgrounds. A few confessed their role in the abuse of others. Some longed to be delivered from their addiction to pornography. A few poured out their bitterness toward God.

Others sought forgiveness from members of the group. Many described failures in their marriages and families. Not a few faced great opposition from church leaders. Some were ready to quit.

And God answered prayer.

Wednesday afternoon it became obvious that there was a significant rift between two groups at the prayer summit. Each group was attempting to "own" the Concert of Prayer movement in their community. Funny, isn't it, how a whole community can become divided over a Concert of Prayer?

Several times men prayed, "Lord, we can't return home with this issue unresolved." Then the prayer would turn to other concerns. A little later one of the men said, "We can't go back home until this issue is dealt with. Let's talk about it." The prayer leader, knowing that a discussion at this point could be extremely divisive, insisted they continue to pray. Finally a man stood and said, "All of us men involved in this controversy know who we are. I suggest we lock ourselves in a room until the issue is resolved." Sixteen men stood and headed down the hall to a meeting room.

For the next hour and a half they met, while the rest prayed their hearts out for reconciliation. Finally the door down the hall opened, and as the sixteen men filed out, they marched into the meeting room singing the doxology at full volume. They stood arm-in-arm and informed the group that total reconciliation had taken place. Wanting to leave no stone unturned, they had listed every failure, everything that had been said and done that needed to be confessed, and then sought forgiveness from each other. They announced that there would be no more prayer summits unless it was agreed upon and supported by the whole group.

During the time the sixteen were seeking reconciliation, two pastors in the large meeting room sought forgiveness from pastors whose churches they had split. There was much rejoicing that day in heaven and upon earth—and much consternation among the forces of hell.

How Do You Sustain a Movement of God?

"United we stand, divided we fall" says it all. And it's probably true.

What would it take to move God's people toward the

unity for which Christ prayed in John 17? For ten years or more I've thought and prayed about what it would take to start and sustain a movement of God in a community. With an emphasis on *sustain*. I keep coming back to unity as the starting point.

But haven't we been there before?

We've all seen how evangelists have drawn leaders together in common cause for a short time. An operational unity developed that enabled a degree of cooperation in a united, city-wide thrust. We applauded it and wondered if such a cooperative mission could be sustained. When the crusade was over, however, it seemed like the local leaders returned to their ruts. Something turned down the divine rheostat. The lights dimmed to normal as the power of a united vision diminished, flickered, and died.

Denominational blinders back in place, leaders gear up again to pursue their own concerns. Like competing dealerships, they do everything in their power to corner the market, to meet their quota, to "evangelize" their fair share . . . and then some. And unity goes AWOL.

The world seems to be better at combining resources in common cause than the church. NATO is a case in point. Facing a common enemy, independent nations have joined ranks to ensure stability and peace. The French have their Mirage Jets, the British their Harriers. The Americans prefer F-14s and 15s. Yet the various weapon systems have been standardized so that there is a coordinated, complementary, interchangeable supply to draw upon. And they regularly participate in joint military exercises under a unified command. Battle plans are already agreed upon should war break out.

What's the battle plan for the church? John 17 lays

out Christ's strategy for members of his army.

Commander Christ places unity at the heart of his military operation. His troops are to stand undivided. Four times he asks his father to enable believers to achieve this difficult objective. Why?

Unity releases power.

Unity attracts the blessing of God.

Unity captures the attention of an unbelieving world. Psalm 133 reads:

How good and pleasant it is when brothers live together in unity . . . For there the LORD bestows [commands] his blessing (1,3).

Where does the Lord command his blessing? Where does he direct his enablement? In what kind of an environment does he release his power?

Where there is unity.

Christ's prayer for his rag-tag army is one of the hinge-points of human history. It's a revolutionary prayer, uttered by one who intends to unleash exactly that—a revolution. It's a neglected prayer whose time has come. It's a prayer about how God wants to use his children to impact their world with the glorious gospel. Please note that the goal for all believers is unity; evangelism is a by-product.

How revealing that the word *world* occurs eighteen times in the prayer and *glory* nine times. Clearly, a lost world is at the heart of the prayer. Christ wants to get his glory and the world together. Consequently, the world must be the focus of our mission. The purpose of our mission is to glorify God in the world in such a way that God's Word is believed, accepted, and obeyed.

Though many themes run through this wartime prayer, evangelism is at its core. "Now this is eternal life," our

Lord prays, "that they may know you . . ." (v. 3). Most of the world doesn't know him. That's the whole issue.

An Enemy Opposes Us

Unfortunately, there's an enemy who opposes our efforts. An evil being stalks the fields of the world, sowing his own perverted gospel. The vast majority of things that impact and shape the thinking of our culture come under his control. Furthermore, this evil one sends his "birds" to steal away the impact of the "good seed" (Matthew 13).

But that's not all. The followers of Satan, the "god" of this world, hate the followers of Christ (John 17:14). That's not good news. The term world [cosmos] usually refers to an organized system, controlled by Satan, which opposes the purposes and programs of God. Our experience confirms this definition. We wrestle, Paul reminds us, not against flesh and blood, but against the ruling powers of hell (Ephesians 6:12). Satan is the great enemy of unity, the architect of chaos and discord.

We need divine protection from this enemy.

In the context of praying for unity, three times Christ prays for our protection. Everything that is good, right, and godly will be opposed. Specifically, Christ is praying against all that would keep his blood-bought ones from living and functioning in complete harmony.

"Protect them," he prays, ". . . so that they may be one as we are one" (v. 11). He presupposes that if protection isn't given, the evil one will be successful in dividing and separating the army of God.

It happened in the Garden. The devil split the first family.

It happened in Israel. He spit the second family.

Whenever it happens, the army loses its corporate impact and becomes a splintered group of beleaguered, ecclesiastical, sheep-stealing fiefdoms. And so we tilt at windmills! It's a shame that often we must wear the Ephesians 6 armor to protect us from other members of the Body of Christ.

Uncommon Praying

I shared a speaking assignment with a dear brother who is a great man of prayer. He was praying for his city on the presumption that he knew how to pray concerning it. God rebuked him for that presumption and asked him why he was not praying that:

its economy would collapse.

the criminal element would surface.

corruption would prevail.

law and order would break down.

division and strife would be unleashed.

the church would undergo persecution.

God seemed to be saying to him, "Call down the bombs upon yourself. And live a godly life in the midst of it all. If you've got the real disease, it will show. If the Body of Christ is anything different than a local library committee, it will show!"

Perhaps we should not presume to know how to pray for our cities. Lord, teach us to pray!

One thing seems obvious. The success of Christ's redemptive mission is greatly dependent upon his people responding under pressure in such a way that the "cosmopolitans" ask Christians the reason for the hope which lies within them. To any serious observer, the situation of the first Christians was anything but hopeful.

Though the future held little hope for them, their

unity, their daily care for each other rocked the Roman Empire. Is it any wonder God added daily to their numbers those who were being saved? At the mercy of Rome with its satanically crazed Caesars, those first pilgrims of the church stood firm.

Notice again whom Christ declares to be the ultimate enemy: "My prayer is not that you take them out of the world, but that you protect them from the evil one." And who is that? The one who:

blew out the lights in Eden.

divided the kingdom of Israel.

lies, deceives, and destroys.

opposes Christian unity.

corrupts the environment in which we live.

sows unbelief in every direction.

But if the Lord doesn't want his Father to take us "out of the world," how do we relate to the world's culture?

Our Relationship to the World System

Three times in John 17 the term *world* is used with different Greek prepositions to describe the believer's relationship to this satanically-dominated system. Christ teaches us that believers are:

out from the world. This is our *position*.

in the world. This is our *location*.

into the world. This is our *vocation*.

First, believers are "out from" the world (*ek*). "I have revealed you to those whom you gave me out of the world" (v. 6). The Lord is not talking about geography. He is talking about the believer's separation from the world system at the point of conversion. We are "delivered out of the kingdom of darkness and translated into the kingdom of light."

Here the Lord is referring to our *position*. Believers are "seated in the heavenlies, far above all principalities and powers." We are delivered out from the dominion and authority of the evil one and his principalities. Satan no longer has authority over our lives. Seated with Christ, we are beyond the control of the adversary. It is this deliverance from satanic control that enables us to successfully penetrate the cosmos and take captives for Christ.

Second, believers are in (*en*) the world. This speaks of our *location*. Jesus said, "I will remain in the world no longer, but they are still in (*en*) the world" (v. 11). Because of our exalted position, we can live successfully wherever we are. "My prayer," our Lord adds, "is not that you take them out of the world but that you protect them from the evil one" (v. 15). We need protection, not relocation. The wheat and tares are to grow up together (Matthew 13). Though we may be tempted to flee, even monastery walls cannot keep the cosmos out. Furthermore, biblical separation is not isolation. Though Satan's authority was broken at the cross, he still remains a formidable foe.

Finally, believers are sent "into (*eis*) the world" (v. 18). This is our vocation. "As you sent me into the world," our Lord said, "I have sent them into (*eis*) the world." It is a corporate sending. He sends "them." Thus deployed, we are under divine commission to penetrate its defenses and take captives.

When this divine commission is taken seriously, it becomes the greatest deterrent to sin. We are sent to reveal his glory. We are sent to corporately model the unity displayed within the Trinity as its members relate to each other and the universe they created. Within the Trinity there is:

unity of purpose.
no competition or jealousy.
a desire to honor and uplift each other.
no sense of possessiveness.
a union of heart and mind.
equality.
diversity within unity.
total commitment to each other.
intellectual agreement.
willing subordination.
complete purity and integrity.
sacrifice.
love.
glory, which is the sum total of all the above.

Spreading the Glory Around

The word *glory* occurs nine times in John 17. Somehow the glory of God and the world are to get together. Unless God "crowns us with glory," we have none, and other than the glory of nature, the world sees none. Ours is to reveal his glory. The usage of the term "glory" in John 17 highlights two important thoughts.

First, we can bring glory to God. What an incredible idea! As our Lord communed with his Father he said, "and glory has come to me through them" (v. 10). What Christ did in them, what was accomplished through them, was a matter of public record.

Second, we bring glory to him by doing what God has called us to do. Christ is our model. He said, "I have brought you [His father] glory on earth by completing the work you gave me to do" (v. 4). We, too, bring glory to God by being what he has created us to be and by doing what he has called us to do. Notice what he did:

I have revealed you to those whom you gave me . . . (v. 6).

I gave them the words you gave me and they accepted them (v. 8).

I protected them and kept them safe (v. 12).

I have sent them into the world . . . (v. 18).

Look at the list. Christ evangelized, discipled, and deployed people out into the world. As "imitators of God," we too are called to reach, win, train, and send believers to penetrate their webs of relationships with the gospel of God's saving grace.

Some Baptists do this. So do some Presbyterians, charismatics and noncharismatics. Most do it within the confines of their own group. Few believers within these groups think, pray, and act corporately. It's foreign to their way of thinking. Within the broader Body of Christ there is little evidence of church leaders coming together and deciding how they can join forces in an ongoing effort to extend the kingdom of light over the kingdom of darkness. Instead, it's "every man for himself."

Consequently, the "cosmopolitan" sees little evidence of divinely-enabled oneness. Considering the odds against unity, its presence would be unique enough to warrant a second look.

How Do We Reveal God's Glory?

God is glorified as we pursue and accomplish his agenda for our lives. And believers committed to his agenda should get along!

But how do believers reveal the glory of God to the cosmos?

First, by coming under the divine commission. "As

you sent me into the world, I have sent them into the world" (v. 18). We all know the great commission. We all know we are to present ourselves as living sacrifices, and our "members" as instruments of righteousness. We know we are to dwell together in unity. We just don't do it because:

denominational headquarters would oppose it.

we're kingdom builders.

we're basically self-centered.

we're victims of past wrongs.

we don't forgive or forget easily.

we have our quotas to fill, our goals to reach, our positions to fill.

we have memories of past failures. We've been burned.

we have theological sacred cows we can't let out to pasture.

we have fellow believers looking over our shoulders.

we fear competition.

we've never done it.

we don't know where to start.

we are prisoners of others' expectations.

we're afraid.

But none of these reasons destroy the thrust of our Lord's prayer. Anything that blunts that thrust must be eliminated.

Second, we reveal the glory of God to the universe by maintaining a divine community. There are two purpose or result clauses in John 17 that underscore the impact of unity upon the unbelieving community.

May they be in us [one] so that [purpose/result] the world may believe that you have sent me (v. 21).

May they be brought to complete unity [purpose or

result] to let the world know that you sent me and have loved them even as you have loved me (v. 23).

Let them be one, the Lord prays, so that the world may be evangelized.

Be a divine community, a united, worldwide family, and the world will get the message that God sent Christ and that he loves the lost.

So how are we doing? On page 8 of the Lausanne Manifesto it says:

> We are ashamed of the suspicions and rivalries, the dogmatism over non-essentials, the power struggles and empire building which spoil our evangelistic witness. We affirm that cooperation in evangelism is indispensable, first because it is the will of God, but also because the doctrine of reconciliation is discredited by our disunity, and because, if the task of world evangelization is ever to be accomplished, we must engage in it together.

We need a breakthrough! We need to consider again the ways in which God reveals his glory.

6.

"... and people have used it for a latrine to this day" (2 Kings 10:27).

GLORY ON DISPLAY: God's Ongoing Media Campaign

R eally.

It's doubtful Samaria, capital of the Northern Kingdom, needed another public restroom. But this one was unique. King Jehu saw to that. Under divine mandate to rid Israel of its idolatry, he came up with a wonderfully creative solution. He hosted a convention for the priests of Baal. "Call an assembly," commanded the king, "in honor of Baal" (2 Kings 10:20). Invitations bearing the seal of the king were sent to the farthest corners of Israel.

All the ministers of Baal showed up. Who could resist the opportunity to honor Baal in the heart of Yahweh-country? "They crowded into the temple of Baal until it was full from one end to the other" (2 Kings 10:21). It was a standing-room-only event. No doubt chariots were double-parked all around the place. The packed temple hummed with excitement. Can you imagine their anticipation? The king himself was hosting this praise festival.

Once the crowd quieted down, Jehu asked the priests of Baal to check out the guest list to be sure no servants of the Lord had crashed the party—no rival priests should be allowed to throw a damper on this special day.

To add to the festivity, the keeper of the wardrobe was commanded to bring out special robes for all the worshipers of Baal. A nice touch! A souvenir, no less. They looked like the First Baptist Church Choir. Thus attired, they surrounded the altar in anticipation as Jehu himself kicked off the get-together by offering the first sacrifice.

But the next event wasn't listed on the convention program.

Eighty armed men burst into the temple and slaughtered all the priests of Baal. None escaped. "Just get the ones with the choir robes." That's all it took.

> The guards and officers threw the bodies out and then entered the inner shrine of the temple of Baal. They brought the sacred stone out of the temple of Baal and burned it. They demolished the sacred stone of Baal and tore down the temple . . . and people have used it for a latrine to this day (2 Kings 10:25-27).

Look at the verbs: They threw the bodies out . . . brought the sacred stone out and burned it . . . demolished the sacred stone of Baal . . . and tore down the temple. . . .

Coldly, methodically, without mercy these religious leaders were put to death. So, we are told, "Jehu destroyed Baal worship in Israel" (2 Kings 10:28).

So what's wrong with letting some of the folks worship Baal?

And why would holy Scripture make a point of reminding us that the ruins of Baal's temple became a toilet? Actually, it's not too difficult to understand the significance of "Baal's Bathroom." It is a supreme insult to urinate on someone or something. I pity the poor soul who would be foolish enough to urinate on the American Flag at a Green Beret convention.

In the case of the disgraced temple of Baal, perhaps urination was a reminder, an act of theological expression, an opportunity to underscore the fact that false gods deserve nothing better. God will not share his glory—or a temple, for that matter—with another. He hasn't changed one bit.

Jehu's Dramatic Statement

The end result of Jehu's creative convention was that Baal's temple became a pile of salty rubbish. It served as a daily reminder that Baal was banished, that the worship of Baal was a stench, that Yahweh was the one true God and will not share his glory with another.

Furthermore, he will not allow an image to be constructed and construed as something to be venerated. His plan never included marketing himself through national, community, or household idols.

Idols are static, God is dynamic.

Idols are man-made, God made man.

Idols are impotent, God is omnipotent.

Idols are one-dimensional, God is multi-dimensional.

Idols are inanimate, God is the source of all animation.

Idols cannot transcend the idol-maker.

Idols are linked with the demonic.

A hand-carved image with a perpetual smile misrepresents God. One could conclude that such a cheshire-deity is unconcerned about injustice and sin. He just sits around and grins. In like manner, a scowling, angered, frozen-frowned idol, the personification of wrath, cannot convey God's mercy and grace.

Most importantly, God has gone on record that idolatry,

the practice of worshiping idols, is wicked. Idols are instruments of satanic deceit.

Idolatry stinks!

Make no mistake about it, Jehu created a tempest in a temple. The continuing presence of that pagan temple was a blight on the spiritual landscape of Israel. Once destroyed, its ruins underscored the impotence of its god. After all, it was at the temple that one went to meet his god and commune with him. Baal wasn't much to worry about if he couldn't even protect his temple. Especially one that was being desecrated hourly.

The Message of Jehu

Why mention Jehu and his Baal Busters? Gods, it seems, want to be known.

If you were invisible as God is, and wanted to communicate, what would you do?

In order to make himself known, God chose to live among his people and reveal himself to them. A vital part of God's communication strategy was to inhabit hand-picked, earthly real estate. Such as:

a holy land,

a holy city,

a holy temple,

and a holy ark.

Only God's presence can make a land, a city, a temple, an ark (or his church) holy. In times past, God chose to reveal his glory through these institutions. For a large part of salvation history the success of God's redemptive mission was related to the condition, maintenance and visibility of these divinely appointed institutions. It's as simple as this: If they obeyed, the world was evangelized! If they obeyed, they were invincible.

The Message of the Lost Ark

Under the wicked leadership of Eli's sons, the Ark of the Covenant was captured by the Philistines. With a note of triumph they placed their newly acquired trophy in the temple of their God, Dagon. It made sense. Hadn't their God prevailed over the God of Israel?

Much to their consternation, however, the next morning their idol Dagon was lying prostrate before the Ark in what could be construed as a posture of worship. It was a huge embarrassment. The local news stations weren't quite sure who to interview or what to blame for this strange turn of events.

What happened? God Almighty said the word and Dagon bit the dust. It was a visual aid whose meaning was clear. But the lessons didn't stop there. That dislocated acacia-wood box continued to stir up trouble. Judgment fell upon every community that hosted the peripatetic ark. Thoroughly upstaged in this divine duel, the Philistine Dagonites tossed in the towel, conceded defeat, put the box on a cart, and tagged a couple of cows to tow it home.

The Crucial Place of Jerusalem

Somewhere in eternity past, God spun the globe between his fingers, thought about it, and selected Jerusalem as his Holy City, the place of his dwelling among men, the place where righteousness could become visible through his people. There Solomon built his temple. There the Ark of the Covenant found its final resting place.

But God's presence was no guarantee that his temple and his city would be protected from the inroads of paganism. Nor was this elaborate structure any guarantee

God would stick around. His presence, availability, and blessings were predicated upon obedience.

The conditions of the land, the city, and the temple were barometers of Israel's spiritual health. In the pagan world, a god who couldn't keep the walls of his city in shape wasn't to be taken seriously. All things being equal, it wasn't an unreasonable perspective. After Nebuchadnezzar leveled Jerusalem and her temple, the surrounding nations symbolically "urinated" on the temple of Yahweh. Listen to their derision:

> All who pass your way
> clap their hands at you;
> they scoff and shake their heads
> at the Daughter of Jerusalem:
> "Is this the city that was called
> the perfection of beauty,
> the joy of the whole earth?"
> (Lamentations 2:15).

Yeah, it was.

Imagine a city being called the "perfection of beauty, the joy of the whole earth." Imagine her people having that kind of reputation! Note that she was called the "joy of the *whole earth*." And so she was . . . for awhile. Jerusalem was never a major banking center or a world-class city of commerce. Her claim to fame was her beauty and joy. In those days if you told a travel agency you wanted to do worship, they'd send you up to Jerusalem. Their joyful praise and worship of Yahweh, their feasts and celebrations captured the attention of the pagan world.

In a very real sense, true worshipers are invincible. It was Israel's spiritual defection, her worship of pagan gods that allowed pagans to breach Jerusalem's walls. What these pagans didn't know was that:

The LORD has done what he planned;
he has fulfilled his word,
which he decreed long ago.
He has overthrown you [Jerusalem] without pity,
he has let the enemy gloat over you,
he has exalted the horn of your foes
(Lamentations 2:17).

God's in charge whether he is honored or not. His sovereignty is unconditional. His presence and blessing are the conditional components of his relationship with his people. Even God's chosen people experience his judgment when they fail to worship him in sincerity and truth.

A Place for God to Display His Glory

In a previous chapter we chronicled something of the horrible civil war that raged between Israel and Judah. Brother against brother. As a result, for much of Jerusalem's history, the world considered the city nothing more than an object of derision.

But God has always taken Jerusalem seriously.

Although he cannot be limited to or contained in this humble planet, he has chosen to be identified with an insignificant part of its real estate. Apparently it's not enough that its heavens declare his glory and the earth displays his creative handiwork. Observe what God said about Jerusalem, the city of David.

I have chosen Jerusalem for my Name to be there (2 Chronicles 6:6).

This city you have chosen (2 Chronicles 6:34).

The city where I chose to put my Name (1 Kings 11:36).

I will reject Jerusalem, the city I chose, and this temple, about which I said, "There shall my Name be" (2 Kings 23:27).

Note that each passage refers to God's choice of Jerusalem. Of all the cities of the earth, God chose to link up with her. We have no record of God residing in any other locale. She became his earthly address, the place where he met with his people. It wasn't, however, the glory of an earthly residence that kept God available and accessible to his people. Divine proximity and protection was conditioned upon the spiritual condition of her citizens. Note that apostasy precluded blessing, idolatry brought judgment, repentance brought restoration.

Jerusalem has sinned greatly (Lamentations 1:8).

This city must be punished; it is filled with oppression (Jeremiah 6:6).

The LORD determined to tear down the wall (Lamentations 2:8).

Jerusalem will become a heap of rubble (Jeremiah 26:18).

All her gateways are desolate (Lamentations 1:4).

All the splendor has departed (Lamentations 1:6).

She saw pagan nations enter her sanctuary (Lamentations 1:10).

They set fire to God's temple and broke down the wall of Jerusalem (2 Chronicles 36:19).

He [Nebuchadnezzar, king of Babylon] carried into exile to Babylon the remnant, who escaped from the sword (2 Chronicles 36:20).

Nehemiah understood the significance of Jerusalem's

desecration. He saw the hidden war going on behind the war machines of the nations.

> Come, let us [those who returned from captivity] rebuild the wall of Jerusalem, and we will no longer be in disgrace (Nehemiah 2:17).

> So the wall was completed in fifty-two days (Nehemiah 6:15).

What can we conclude? Because of sin and failure, God withdrew his protective hand from Jerusalem for a time. Yes, "the Glory of God departed." But God's plans for Jerusalem haven't been abandoned.

The apostle John summarizes her future by reminding us that someday a New Jerusalem, the Holy City, will come down from heaven. He wrote:

> And I heard a loud voice from the throne saying, "Now the dwelling of God is with men, and he will live with them. They will be his people, and God himself will be with them and be their God" (Revelation 21:3).

Where did God dwell with men? In Jerusalem. Where will God dwell among men? In Jerusalem.

It is clear that God chose Jerusalem as his earthly residence, as his capitol, the place where his name is to be enthroned. King Cyrus referred to God as "the God who is in Jerusalem" (Ezra 1:3). So what was God's address in Jerusalem? The Temple.

> Your son [Solomon] . . . will build the temple for my Name (1 Kings 5:5).

> I have chosen and consecrated this temple so that my Name may be there forever. My eyes and my heart will always be there (2 Chronicles 7:16).

The Lord promised Solomon and his generation that:

> If you follow my decrees . . . I will live among the
> Israelites and will not abandon my people Israel
> (1 Kings 6:12-13).

Should Israel be disobedient and eventually end up in captivity in a foreign land, they are instructed to pray:

> toward the land you gave their fathers,
> toward the city you have chosen and
> toward the temple (2 Chronicles 6:38).

Although Solomon's temple differed greatly from the portable Tabernacle of Moses, it shared essential components with it. That's where the similarity ended. No monarch before or after has had such an expensive, magnificent temple. Its very presence was a theological statement.

Everything was present for Israel to demonstrate to the world what God-flavored people are like. They had the law, the sacrificial system, a consecrated priesthood, and a present, caring God. All that was necessary to deal with their sin was in place. And, as Solomon said, "there is no one who does not sin" (2 Chronicles 6:36).

It was equally important that God had a residence—a city, a temple from which to beam his glory into the darkened corners of the earth. His marketing plan involved displaying his glory through the distinctives of those who honored his name and worshiped at his temple.

Did the message of Yahweh's sovereignty and power penetrate the pagan world? Absolutely. There was a period in the history of Jerusalem when the earth's nations believed that the city of David was invincible.

> The kings of the earth did not believe, nor did any
> of the world's people, that enemies and foes could

enter the gates of Jerusalem (Lamentations 4:12).

The mightiest army could not prevail against it. Would to God that the church had that kind of reputation!

The Holy City's invincibility had little to do with its fortifications and military prowess. It had everything to do with the character and activity of the God who "dwelt with" her. The message of God's power and might, the truth about his holiness was gossiped about the known world—by divine design.

Jerusalem could only fall from within. No king, no armies, no display of military might could touch her as long as she wholeheartedly followed Yahweh. Theological drift and a pit-driven "ecumenism" were always Israel's greatest dangers. There are absolutes which cannot be surrendered without great peril.

No wonder Jehu became a Baal buster.

When the flag of Yahweh flew over his chosen residence, things went well with Israel. They experienced peace and prosperity. But the impact of Israel's godliness went beyond divine protection and prosperity.

The Worldwide Implications of the Temple

Solomon understood the spiritual implications of the city and its temple. It was a temple for all mankind. Solomon's prayer of dedication reveals his insight into the redemptive implications of God's earthly residence.

Solomon had the heart of an evangelist! He was concerned that the 153,600 aliens living in Israel and tourists from other lands might know that the temple he built was the residence of Almighty God. To this end he prays:

As for the foreigner who does not belong to your

people Israel but has come from a distant land
because of [note three things]

your great name and
your mighty hand and
your outstretched arm

when he comes and prays toward this temple, then
hear from heaven, your dwelling place, and do
whatever the foreigner asks of you, *so that all the
peoples of the earth may know your name and fear
you*, as do your own people Israel, and may know
that this house I have built bears your Name
(2 Chronicles 6:32-33).

Solomon hits the bull's-eye. They will come from distant lands to the holy city, to the temple if they hear
about Yahweh's:

reputation—his great name.

power and authority—his mighty hand.

mercy—his outstretched arm.

"Answer their prayers, Lord, so that they may know
your name and fear you." Solomon's talking about evangelism. He's suggesting a strategy to convince the foreigner that Yahweh is God and is to be feared.

Interesting in the light of today's debate over "signs
and wonders" is Solomon's request that God answer the
prayer of the alien so he will become a believer. "Grant
him the desire of his heart, forgive him, do something
wonderful for him so that he may know and fear you."

But it all goes up in smoke if Israel abandons Yahweh.
And she did.

Eventually Jerusalem, the residence of Yahweh-God,
was overrun by the enemy. Jeremiah explains that:

It happened because of the sins of her prophets and
the iniquities of her priests . . . (Lamentations 4:13).

As the religious leaders, so the nation. It's the same today.

A Foreigner Searches for God

Note that the foreigner comes from a distant land. He's on a theological quest, a search for the one, true God. He's heard about the God who dwells among his people, who is attentive to their cry, who delivers his people from their enemies. He knew about the Red Sea and the conquest of Canaan. Note that he comes to "pray toward the temple." He's had it with the false gods of his own people.

He anticipates that the Bride of God will be an earthly extension of his splendor, the incarnation of righteousness. Shouldn't people be like their God? That is a reasonable expectation. Imagine him arriving at Jerusalem, the capitol of Yahweh-Elohim, and observing altars to pagan gods on every street corner. Imagine his disillusionment in discovering they are worshiping the same pagan, impotent gods of his own people. Or, they "worship" the true God, but are pagans at heart.

Worse yet, imagine his pilgrimage ending as he approaches the holy city and sees its gates burned and walls in ruins. Would he not reasonably conclude, on the basis of physical evidence, that Yahweh was either a paper deity or had somehow died?

It was not to have been this way. Instead, having observed God's protection of his loyal subjects, the alien should have come to pray toward his temple. Through answered prayer, Solomon reasons, the alien will become a believer, a follower of Yahweh. Under the banner of their God, the Israelites did the impossible. Their God doesn't change.

His people, however, do. And when they do, the enemies sense their decline, the breaking down of morality, the loss of character, the rise of crime and corruption. And they close in for the kill.

How Disobedience Thwarts Evangelism

Solomon's prayer was a good one. Its basic assumptions are correct. But Israel's apostasy and civil wars cut the heart out of it. Civil war didn't impress the aliens. It never does.

There was a time when Israel's enemies would not dare attack the capital city. But when her people fell into gross sin, the equation changed. Listen to the sarcasm of Sennacherib, king of Assyria, as he taunts Israel and makes fun of her god:

Now do not let Hezekiah deceive you and mislead you like this. Do not believe him, for no god of any nation or kingdom has been able to deliver his people from my hand or the hand of my fathers. How much less will your god deliver you from my hand! (2 Chronicles 32:15).

Do not let Hezekiah persuade you to trust in the LORD (2 Kings 18:30).

How then can the LORD deliver Jerusalem from my hand? (2 Kings 18:35).

Choose life and not death! (2 Kings 18:32).

The king also wrote letters insulting the LORD, the God of Israel (2 Chronicles 32:17).

Sennacherib also sent his field commander to "ridicule the living God" (2 Kings 19:4). Among other things, he claimed that "the LORD himself told me to march against this country and destroy it" (2 Kings 18:25).

Sennacherib's threats were not to be taken lightly. He'd already captured Samaria, capital of Israel and taken the Northern Kingdom into captivity. Now he turned against Judah, the Southern Kingdom, and captured all its fortified cities. Hezekiah bought him off for a time by sending him gold and silver from the temple treasury. Furthermore, he

> stripped off the gold with which he had covered the doors and doorposts of the temple of the LORD, and gave it to the king of Assyria (2 Kings 18:16).

Now word comes that the Assyrians are moving toward Jerusalem. Hezekiah tore his clothes, put on sackcloth and went to the temple of the Lord.

> Give ear, O LORD, and hear; open your eyes, O LORD, and see; listen to the words Sennacherib has sent to insult the living God (2 Kings 19:16).

Why could the enemy get away with insulting Almighty God? Why does the enemy succeed in mocking God? Because obedience, godliness, and unity are the weapons of God's children. *When they are absent, God allows the enemy to prevail.*

Hezekiah knew the issues were spiritual, not physical. It would take unconventional warfare for Judah to triumph. God had not acted to deliver the Northern Kingdom from the hands of the Assyrians. Was not Judah's sister, Israel, defeated "because they had not obeyed the LORD their God" (2 Kings 18:12)?

You know how the story ends. While Sennacherib's immediate threat is smashed, ultimately Jerusalem is destroyed by the Babylonians. Judah is taken into captivity.

The temple is destroyed and its treasures carted away to foreign lands.

God's New Post Office Box

And God no longer has an earthly address? Wrong. He has, however, chosen not to live in man-made edifices. Something new, something wonderful has happened. He no longer inhabits temples made by human hands.

> The God who made the world and everything in it is the Lord of heaven and earth and *does not live in temples built by hands* (Acts 17:24, emphasis mine).

So where does he now live? He dwells in the lives of individual believers.

> Don't you know that you yourselves are God's temple and that God's Spirit lives in you? (1 Corinthians 3:16).

> Do you not know that your body is a temple of the Holy Spirit, who is in you, whom you have received from God? (1 Corinthians 6:19).

Where does he now live? He indwells the church. For *we are the temple of the living God*. As God has said:

> "I will live with them and walk among them, and I will be their God, and they will be my people" (2 Corinthians 6:16).

Ephesians 2:21-22 underscores this wonderful truth.

> In him [Christ] *the whole building* [the church] is joined together and rises to become a holy temple in the Lord. *And in him you too are being built together to become a dwelling in which God lives by his Spirit* (emphasis mine).

Like Israel of old, the quality of our corporate life is the key to the evangelization of our communities and our world.

The land, the city, the temple, the ark. Ichabod. Quality control broke down and "the glory of God departed." With Christ as its center, a new building is joined together to become the new residence of God among his people. It happens as believers are "built together." The Greek verb "built together" means to "be built in company with something." Its passive voice indicates that we are not doing the building, but that God as agent is joining us together to be a dwelling place of God.

Believers from the Presbyterians and Baptists, the Methodists and Assemblies of God, all true builders, are being joined together by God into a dwelling place of God. We are the means through which God reveals his glory . . . if we keep the walls up, the gates in good repair, and don't fall from within.

The goal of the Church, the Body of Christ in action, is to build up the house of the Lord through evangelism and edification. If the true dwelling place of God breaks forth in our cities, great revival will break out.

What God has joined together, let no man put asunder! His communication strategy is to wrap ideas in people!

Paul served the Corinthians a strong warning. "If anyone destroys God's temple [a church], God will destroy him; for God's temple is sacred." I believe Paul is talking about one who would destroy the unity of a local church. The surrounding context refers to the problem of divisions in the church. When Christians divide into warring camps of divisive, sectarian groups, they destroy the power and impact of the Body of Christ.

All things, we are told, are to be done decently and in order. God does not dwell in ruins. The Old Testament makes it patent God will neither dwell in or sanction with power any group that remains in a fallen, disobedient condition. On the other hand, when Israel or the Church marches to the beat of God's will, they have the backing of and can minister under the authority of Christ.

> Unless the LORD builds the house, its builders labor in vain. Unless the LORD watches over the city, the watchmen stand guard in vain (Psalm 127:1).

Francis Frangipane claims "It will take a citywide church to win a citywide war." Our Lord warns that "every city or household divided against itself *will not* stand" (Matthew 12:25). In other words, where disunity reigns, don't expect the Lord to build his house or guard the city.

Why should it surprise us if the Church, like Baal's Temple, becomes a modern day "cultural bathroom" and is treated with contempt? Or ignored?

God's presence, availability and blessings are predicated upon obedience. Remember that the church at Ephesus was warned that unless they changed, unless they recovered their first love, God would remove his candlestick (Revelation 2:1-11).

Unity is an indispensable key to God's blessing. And that leads us to the next question. Just what are the dimensions of a divinely established unity?

7

UNITAS: The Landscape of Unity

U_{nitas.}

McDonald's has it. Somehow a New York Big Mac looks, feels, and tastes identical to one served in Los Angeles.

The Mormons have it. Stakes and temples dot the landscape. From the Atlantic to the Pacific, cult members are perceived to be unified, squeaky-clean, red, white, and blue patriots who love God, home, family, and apple pie. With relatively few adherents and a ridiculous world view, they out-think, out-plan, out-strategize, and out-market most of the evangelical church.

Why? They're united.

They master-plan their expansion, buying up properties years before a stake is built. They pack school boards, build "seminaries" next to high schools, infiltrate and influence local governments, and go door-to-door selling their diabolical doctrine. And, of course, they care for their own.

Somehow, they speak and act with one voice. They do it together. At least that's how they are perceived. Like it or not, perception is reality!

Unfortunately, few would accuse the true church of having such unity.

It's doubtful the evil one cares whether New York and Los Angeles Big Macs look and taste the same. It stands to reason, however, that he would unify any group that pumps theological fog, distorting the person and work of Christ. Surely he knows that a house divided against itself cannot stand. So he divides the church and unifies the enemies of the gospel, making them both pawns in the accomplishment of his sinister purposes.

Division Can Be God's Idea

At times, division is also part of God's plan. He knows a divided house lacks punch.

The rebellious builders of the Tower of Babel had a satanic vision that God snuffed out. The memory of a universal flood encouraged them to build a tower that would deliver them from the judgment of God and enable them to live as they pleased. Seeking to "reach heaven" to "make a name for themselves," they joined together in a vast and ambitious project. God said:

> If as *one* people speaking the *same* language they have begun to do this, then nothing they plan to do will be impossible for them (Genesis 11:6).

It is significant that God Himself highlights the power of a unified vision. He's saying that if people who are one and on the same wavelength do their homework, nothing will be impossible for them. A unified people with a unified plan of action can become a formidable force—for good or evil.

In this case, God created a verbal traffic jam to disrupt the evil plans of the Babel builders. Please note it was God who divided them. All the skills and resources were there to complete the project. But when God was through with them, they couldn't even communicate, and the project fell apart.

What God did was necessary, for if a united people speak the same language and pursue the same goal, virtually "nothing they plan to do will be impossible for them." Unified vision and unified action are prerequisites for the success of virtually all endeavors.

What would happen if believers, walking by means of the Holy Spirit, united themselves around the project of reaching a lost community? Is it possible that "nothing they plan . . . will be impossible for them"?

Union Doesn't Guarantee Unity

Tie two cats together by the tails and toss them over a clothesline. I suppose you'd have union, but you wouldn't have unity. Most likely they would fight like, well, cats and cats.

Must they fight? Could there be unity?

Isn't it likely these felines would be unified in their belief that tying tails together is an inappropriate activity? So knotted together, surely they would be unanimous in their desire for deliverance. Certainly such conceptual unity is a good place to begin! They both want off the clothesline!

In discussing their dilemma, they might even discover they like each other. Perhaps their predicament would drive them to stoop so low as to seek help from the tail-wagging canine corps. Could they come up with a tactical plan of escape based on their cooperation? Once escaped, could they stay unified until they wreaked havoc upon their enemies?

My cat-and-dog story suggests one critical idea: Unity has several flavors that involve attitude as well as action. In fact, there are many different ways in which unity expresses itself.

We can be unified in our worship.

We can be unified in our belief systems.

We can join together around biblically appropriate behavior.

We can be one in our relationships with other like-minded people.

We can be ethnically reconciled.

We can join together in common cause.

Christ is not divided. Scripture reminds us that "if you have any encouragement from being united with Christ [union] then . . . [be] like-minded [unity]." Note again, for the sake of the record, that true unity is based on union! Virtually no community of born-again people will experience the full power of the Spirit's anointing until, impelled by the Spirit, they become one in heart and soul.

Boiled down to its essence, unity means agreement. Can two walk together unless they be agreed? Agreed about what? Does unity mean we must all:

- be dispensationalists?
- worship the same way?
- use the same Bible translation?
- like organ music?
- be Calvinists?
- give altar calls?
- agree on political issues?
- be pre-tribulationalists?
- be Charismatics?
- raise our hands in worship?
- speak in tongues?
- break bread every Sunday?
- use the same mode of baptism?

No, we don't need to be in agreement over the above list. But how about the following list? Does unity mean we must all:

- believe in the deity and humanity of Christ?
- believe in the inspiration and authority of Scripture?
- believe in the Trinity?
- believe in salvation by faith alone?
- believe in the substitutionary atonement?
- believe in holiness of life?
- believe in the unity of the Body?
- believe we are members one of another?
- believe in the reality of Satan?
- believe in salvation in Christ alone?
- believe in the bodily resurrection of Christ?
- believe in the bodily return of Christ?

Though most believers would have differences of opinion over the first list, they'd embrace the second one. Certainly there are some critical areas of agreement that are essential to the cause of Christ and the coming of his kingdom. Paul himself warned of dire consequences for anyone who preached another gospel (Galatians 1:8,9). John warned against false teachers who deny the humanity and deity of Christ (1 John 2:22; 4:2-3). Beware of wolves in sheep's clothing!

Those same false shepherds are alive and well in today's church. They are not joined to Christ or to the Body of Christ. We have no basis of unity with such traitors to the faith. These we are to oppose and expose.

But in each community, there is a "critical mass" of laity and clergy, who, if unified, could impact the rest of the church and make great inroads into the unbelieving world. If John 17 is true, there is little chance of impact unless those who name the name of Christ move toward unity.

Who Leads the Pack?

If what I have said is true, the question begs to be asked: Who should be leading the pack toward biblical unity?

Listen to Paul. He reminds the believers in Ephesus that God appointed "some to be apostles, some to be prophets, some to be evangelists, and some to be pastors and teachers . . . so that the body of Christ may be built up *until we all reach unity in the faith*" (Ephesians 4:11-13). Note that a major purpose for the placement of gifted communicators in the body is the attainment of unity, which I take to be an agreement about the essentials of faith and life. A conceptual unity, if you please.

Note it well. Gifted men and women are given to build up the church in the direction of unity. If anyone can and should lead us to biblical unity, it's those folks. If they don't do it, no one will.

Conceptual Unity

Is it likely that believers will ever be in complete theological agreement? Not in this life. I've found it helpful to remind myself that not all doctrines are of equal importance. Some are more essential than others. If that were not true, our Lord would not have answered the question about "which command is the greatest" (*see* Matthew 22:35ff).

I doubt that most believers would consider the debate over the modes of baptism as important as the doctrine of the deity of Christ or the virgin birth. Few (I would hope) would separate from other believers over issues of church polity or the gifts of the Spirit.

An interesting phenomenon takes place when pastors and leaders spend four to five days together in the presence of the Lord. Doctrinal barriers that seem insurmountable fade as believers discover their mutual love for the Savior and his Word.

Much of the "conceptual/theological" division within the church grows out of a failure to distinguish between tradition and biblical theology. Good tradition can become divisive if it is viewed as an essential for faith and practice. Interdenominational cooperation would be greatly enhanced if we could avoid justifying separatistic attitudes by appealing to denominational and cultural tradition.

The goal is not to eliminate tradition, but to acknowledge it as such and avoid making it normative for Christian fellowship. Tradition is an action or belief that seems to hang around, even though it lacks substantial biblical support.

While a tradition may be neutral in itself, it can become errant if it fosters division within the Body of Christ. Paul warns about "vain disputations over words." Any belief that supersedes or nullifies Scripture is certain to encourage disunity.

To counteract the influence of tradition, the reformers came up with the principle of *sola scriptura* (Latin for "Scripture alone!"). All tradition should be subservient to and judged by Scripture alone. It's a wonderful and necessary ideal. In real life, however, the church is shot through with interpretive traditions.

Thus we have the Evangelical Free Tradition, the Methodist Tradition, the Independent Bible Tradition. Some are ruled by elders, other by deacons. Some totally immerse, others sprinkle. Still others have weekly communion while some partake every month. Some adopt a "decision theology," others develop a "nurturing theology." Each one, of course, claims that their practices are based on Scripture alone. So, of course, everyone else is wrong. Believing their distinctives to be "clearly biblical," they impute to them biblical authority.

But is the issue of one ruling elder biblical or cultural? Is passing the plate biblical or cultural? How about only elders serving communion, or worship services meeting mid-morning on Sundays? Or choir robes, stained glass windows, organs, or closed communion? Or hands raised in worship? Or feet washed in basins? Don't forget the clap offerings or praise songs! Or the parachurch organizations!

For many, these and other examples become non-negotiable and any group that differs is viewed as opposing biblical truth. So my charismatic friends find themselves on one side of a theological fence, as the "hand" tries to tell the "foot" it doesn't need to walk.

Christ both affirmed and opposed Jewish traditions. He graced the synagogue with his presence—an institution which cannot trace its origins to the Scriptures. On the other hand, he confronted the Pharisaic tradition of *corban* as described in Mark 7.

Some traditions are useful and beneficial. Others are not. To preserve unity in the midst of conceptual differences, believers need to be aware of their own traditions. They should appreciate those that enhance biblical concepts, even while dispensing with those that conflict with other clear teachings or create division within the Body.

Article XXXIV of the *Thirty-nine Articles of the Church of England* makes this unusual statement:

Every particular or national Church hath authority to ordain, change and abolish, Ceremonies or Rites of the Church ordained only by man's authority, so that all things be done to edifying.

Read it again. All rites based solely on man's authority are subject to review and change if necessary.

Is there a core of orthodoxy, a theological creed around which a conceptual unity could be constructed? Without attempting to construct one, the answer is "yes." Many believe that Paul's list in Ephesians 4 is an ancient theological creed. "Make every effort," he writes, "to keep the unity of the Spirit through the bond of peace (Ephesians 4:2)." Then he spells out seven great biblical truths. There is, he reminds us,

One body:	Ecclesiology
One Spirit:	Pneumatology
One hope:	Eschatology
One Lord:	Christology
One faith:	Soteriology
One baptism:	Soteriology, Pneumatology, Ecclesiology

One God and Father: Theology Proper

One Body. This doctrine eliminates universalism and confronts denominationalism. Those who really believe there is only one body live out the fact that they are "members of one another." As such, our responsibility is to function properly within that body so that it "grows and builds itself up in love, as each part does its work."

One Spirit. Christians are monotheists, not polytheists. We are all indwelt by the same Spirit. The same Spirit teaches us and guides us into truth. This same

Spirit indwells us and conforms us to Christ. The person we refer to as the Holy Spirit is the catalyst for unity within the family of God.

One Hope. All believers share the blessed hope of Christ's return and reign. This hope presupposes that the One who died was raised from the dead and lives today. It is the hope of seeing him whom we love. Though believers would differ on the timing and circumstances of his return, the blessed hope of that return has been a cardinal doctrine of the church since its inception.

One Lord. To this One every knee shall bow and every tongue proclaim his lordship. He is divine. Virgin born, he became a man and in that body was raised from the dead. He is the creator and the redeemer, the object of our devotion, the one to whom we present our bodies a living sacrifice.

One Faith. While there may be many "faiths," Christians through the centuries have proclaimed that there is only "one faith" that is genuine and saving. It is faith in Christ alone. He will not share his glory with another. He alone is the way, the truth, and the life. Believers have been united in their affirmation that "no one comes to the Father except through me [Christ]."

One Baptism. Although the details surrounding the doctrine of the baptizing work of the Spirit may be a subject of debate, Christians acknowledge that there is an act of the Spirit that unites believers in that living organism called the church. Certainly Paul is talking about the "one baptism" that unites, meaning the one that joins us to Christ's Body, the church universal.

One God and Father of All. The orthodox through the centuries have affirmed that there is only one God. This ancient statement of faith includes a trinitarian affirmation: Note the reference to one Father, one Lord, and one Spirit. This God, Paul reminds us, is the Father of all. Certainly he is Father as to source and sustenance. "For in him we live and move and have our being" (Acts 17:28). Likewise, he has the heart of a father. For centuries believers have joined in praying to him as their "heavenly Father."

While not complete or exhaustive, these seven great affirmations form theological boundary conditions. They highlight the great faith "unities" that characterize those who are truly blood-bought believers. Paul's list at least gives us a starting place.

I might add that this core of orthodoxy is a wartime doctrinal statement. The allied forces fight shoulder-to-shoulder because of their commitment to a "wartime" creed, a short summary of commonly shared beliefs and values. As soon as the war ends, these allies will go back to debating the merits of their diverse political, economic, and social structures. When the war between darkness and light is finished, we'll have eternity to debate the nuances of our theological creeds (although I doubt we'll want to). In the meantime, we close ranks and become one.

In light of our need to be like-minded, three questions must be answered.

Question one: What is the essential core of orthodoxy?

Question two: Who adheres to this essential core of orthodoxy?

Question three: What is my responsibility to those who hold to this core of orthodoxy?

These three questions, like those which will follow, are for you to answer—and then, to act upon appropriately.

Doxological Unity

If differing groups share the same purpose, shouldn't they check each other out? If your purpose is doxological—if it is to glorify God in every way possible—and that's my purpose, too, maybe we should get together. All believers are linked in the great redemptive purposes of God. We're linked in our need to worship him whose name is "above all names."

Perhaps common worship is the most powerful unifying experience in the Christian arsenal. Though glorifying God in worship is at the heart of the mission of the church, communities of faith differ greatly over how they worship. Most agree on whom they worship and why. It's the "how" that sometimes creates barriers.

Worship services can be manipulative, self-serving platforms for kingdom builders. People can be used. Spiritual exhibitionists show up in every tradition. These and other realities still do not preclude the necessity for prolonged, serious worship.

The good news is that quality, unhurried time in his presence usually leads to repentance and growth. Furthermore, worshiping with other brothers and sisters confirms the positive, important things we share in common. Many communities are holding joint services that prove to be times of great worship and praise.

In light of our need to worship God in Spirit and in truth, three more questions need to be answered:

Question one: What is the mission and purpose of the church?

Question two: Who is committed to this mission?

Question three: What is my responsibility to those who share this understanding of the purpose of the church?

Behavioral Unity

We are saddened and often angered when we see Christian leaders fall into sin. At such times we are forced to look inward at our own susceptibilities and wonder if we, too, might make some of the same sinful choices. Certainly we are capable of it. Lest we become judgmental, it is good to remind ourselves of our own vulnerability. "Let him that thinks he stands," Paul warns us, "take heed lest he fall."

How do we relate to the disobedient, the kingdom builders, the fallen? Scripture is clear that we are to separate ourselves from those who persist in violating biblical norms. Paul calls us to separate ourselves from adulterers and fornicators within the church. The desired outcome, of course, is repentance and restoration. We are not to join hands with all who name the name of Christ.

> We command you, brothers, to keep away from every brother who is idle and does not live according to the teaching you received from us (2 Thessalonians 3:6).

> But now I am writing you that you must not associate with anyone who calls himself a brother but is sexually immoral or greedy, an idolater or a slanderer, a drunkard or a swindler. With such a man do not even eat (1 Corinthians 5:11).

When we join hands with our allies and face a hostile community, we want to be linked with men and women of like-precious faith. Different, yes. Yet we would oppose associating with those who have not declared themselves, who persist in being carnal, who are sold out to unbiblical priorities.

Yes, there is an appropriate behavior, a Christian

lifestyle. While loosely defined, it is recognized and appreciated. Many pastors in denominations other than your own love and serve the Lord. It is with these that we must link and impact a city for God. God has his remnant in most of the major denominations; laity and clergy whose Christlikeness invites us to join with them in worship and service.

A Nazarene pastor who participated in a Prayer Summit writes:

I hate to use a statement I've heard frequently this week, but it seems to say it best—this has been a life-changing experience because my concept of the Body has been greatly enlarged. What a privilege it will be to spend the rest of my ministry side-by-side with God's chosen men of all denominations.

Another writes:

I'm excited about the unity that is being established in our city and about the *Rumblings of Revival* that I hear and see.

Still another leader writes:

We came away with a feeling of unity that has never before existed among our pastors. We find ourselves united in prayer and heart. We will never be the same. . . . Seems to me God may be preparing the entire Northwest for revival.

Just one more:

It was like a dream come true to have brothers from so many different denominations praying, crying, singing, and celebrating together.

And where are we? We believe . . . we are on the verge of one of the greatest ingatherings of

Christians that the Northwest has ever seen.

The unity we experienced during this prayer summit was an experience we will never forget.

Yes, we are under biblical mandate to link up with those brothers who are living a biblical, Christ-centered lifestyle. Again, we must ask three questions:

Question one: What is a biblical lifestyle?

Question two: Who exhibits godly behavior?

Question three: What is my responsibility to one who exhibits godly behavior?

We can all come up with pastors in some particular denomination who have run off with a secretary. Nonetheless, we are to stand with those who are currently walking with God.

Relational Unity

"Live in harmony with one another," says Paul in Romans 12:16. Wouldn't it be wonderful to move from acceptance and approval to appreciation and admiration? Could we move from duty to true devotion, from formality to friendship?

An Episcopal bishop lives in our neighborhood. He is a radiant Christian, a true brother, and he is becoming a friend. Once we're on the track to unity, let's keep the train rolling toward friendship. God wants his kids to love and enjoy each other, even if we're from different denominations! Again, there are some questions:

Question one: What are the marks of a Christian friend?

Question two: Who exhibits these graces?

Question three: What is my responsibility to a believer who exhibits these graces, who is a potential friend and ally in the faith?

And a reminder: "Each of you should look . . . to the interests of others" (Philippians 2:4).

Ethnic Unity

One of the great blights on Christendom is its lack of ethnic unity. Anyone who is interested in attracting the blessing of God upon a given community must not overlook the need for ethnic reconciliation.

There does not seem to be a statute of limitations on the sins of the past. God sent three years of famine into David's ministry because his predecessor (the previous pastor, if you will) broke a four hundred-year-old treaty and tried to annihilate the Gibeonites. Still, it doesn't sound fair, does it, that my pastorate should experience three years of spiritual famine because of the transgressions of a previous leader?

David went to the Gibeonites and asked what was needed to make restitution. Did they want gold, silver, land? No, they wanted the seven "bloody sons of Saul," the Saddam Husseins of their generation. When these men were put to death, the text says, "God answered prayer in behalf of the land."

In the dozen or so revivals in the Old Testament, about half involved the confession of the sins of the fathers. These revival leaders recognized that the blessing of God would continue to evade them until they owned up to the failures of their ancestors.

Convicted about the lack of reconciliation between blacks and whites in Portland, several of us began meeting with some of our dear black brothers and sisters. Our efforts, just a beginning, climaxed with a wonderful service of reconciliation and celebration involving about fifteen hundred people. It was a great beginning. That morning about fifty black and white churches had a pulpit exchange. I believe God was pleased.

At the reconciliation service, prayers of confession were offered by both blacks and whites. We anticipate this will not only become an annual event, but a growing one. Even as I write this paragraph, I have an appointment this Thursday to begin planning for our next service.

Tactical Unity

It's not enough to just get along. There's more to Christ's kingdom coming than Christians living the Christian life and being friends. There are walls to be rebuilt and gates to be repaired. Vital missions remain dreams until the Body-corporate joins in tactical unity. Is not the Lord's call to unity also a call to significant, unified effort?

Pastors are trained to exegete Scripture. Few, if any, are told how to exegete a community or city. If it's true that every generation needs revival, isn't it important that seminary education deal with the question of how to initiate and sustain revival in a specific, geographically defined area? In seven years of graduate seminary studies I never heard the topic of revival discussed. Nor was interdenominational cooperation ever talked about. There was no discussion about strategizing and working together.

Certainly God doesn't want or intend that *all* new believers in a community attend only one fellowship. Nor is it reasonable to assume that he intends to bring revival to only one church.

The concept of a unified, city-wide strategy is foreign to most of our thinking. And yet our independent, isolated attempts to influence a city will be of little worth.

In fact, when we function alone we fall into the trap of the evil one. Matthew 12:25 reminds us that if the leaders of a city are divided against themselves, *they will not stand*. Conversely, if people respond to the Chief Architect and Builder and fit in with his priorities, their labor will not be in vain and their city will be guarded (Psalm 127:1).

The Lord is clearly "building his house" as believers become the "dwelling of God in the Spirit" (Ephesians 2:19-22). This house is populated with believers who are evangelicals and charismatics, from mainline and independent churches.

What is ultimately the answer to AIDS, the homeless, the substance abusers, the profane, those suffering from physical and spiritual starvation? Mile-High Ministries in Denver may suggest an answer. It's a coalition of a dozen or more fellowships linked to address these issues. They've established food banks, outlet stores, job training programs, and literacy classes. Many are finding Christ through their efforts.

Groups of pastors in towns and cities around the Northwest are meeting regularly to pray and strategize how they can become the "church" of their city and stand together against the forces of darkness. They're not interested in another warmed-over ministerial meeting. Having experienced a Prayer Summit, they desire to come together for fervent prayer and worship. And God is answering prayer.

The whole concept of tactical unity is new territory for most of us. Churches are featuring other ministries in their church bulletins. One pastor drives to two or three other churches early on Sunday mornings and prays that God will bless their ministry of the Word. Many are closing evening services and meeting jointly for a time of prayer, praise, and spiritual warfare.

Others are beginning joint-venture projects to meet specific needs. Some are commissioning couples to minister for a year or two in other needy ministries. And God is pleased and begins to command his blessing.

It's time we learned that the key to ministry is to give it away!

8

HUMILITY: Where Unity Begins

It was a flashy entrance.

When everything about the temple was ready, Solomon invited God to move in. He did.

Now arise, O LORD God, and come to your resting place (2 Chronicles 6:41).

When Solomon finished his prayer, a shaft of fire hurled earthward and consumed the sacrifice. Simultaneously the Lord's matchless glory burst from the temple. With glory cracking and popping everywhere, the priests were glory-frozen in their tracks, unable to enter the temple. When the ordinary folks saw the fire and glory, they hit the deck. Foreheads to the pavement, they worshiped and gave thanks.

As worship services go, it was an extravaganza, the climax of decades of hard work. Though we're unsure of its Arbitron rating, we do know it was a twenty-two-thousand-cattle and a-hundred-and-twenty-thousand-sheep event. I'm sure that put it right at the top of the charts.

In his acceptance speech to Solomon, God said of his new home, "my eyes and my heart will always be here" (2 Chronicles 7:16).

For a couple of weeks they celebrated. All good things, however, must come to an end. So Solomon sent them home

> joyful and glad in heart for the good things the LORD had done for David and Solomon and for his people Israel (2 Chronicles 7:10).

When things had calmed down, God appeared to Solomon one night to discuss some of the fine print about his new housing arrangement. He said:

> I have heard your prayer and have chosen this place for myself as a temple for sacrifices.

So far, so good.

> When I shut up the heavens so that there is no rain, or command locusts to devour the land or send a plague among my people . . . (2 Chronicles 7:12-13).

Not so good. Can you see the frown on Solomon's face? "You're stopping the rain? You're flying in locusts? You're shipping in a plague? Why would you do a thing like that?"

The following context enables us to see that when leaders encounter spiritual drought, devastation, and disease, it's not business as usual. It's time to do business with God. Drought, locusts, and plagues are symptoms of spiritual defection.

Verse 14 contains the roadmap home, the essential components of revival, the steps necessary to initiate a fresh work of God in our midst, a clue to confronting spiritual defection. It's a familiar text.

> If my people, who are called by my name, will humble themselves and pray and seek my face and turn from their wicked ways, then will I hear from

heaven and will forgive their sin and will heal their land (2 Chronicles 7:14).

When the dust is blowing, the locusts are thriving, and folks are dying, read the signs. Wake up. If your spiritual windshield is splattered with grasshoppers, do something about it.

If your heart is barren, something is wrong.

If your homes are coming apart at the seams, something is wrong.

If your leadership team is in a shambles, something is wrong.

If your church isn't growing, something is wrong.

If your church is prayerless, something is wrong.

If your church lacks vision, something is wrong.

If your church is carnal, something is wrong.

If your pride keeps you from doing something about it, something is wrong.

If any of the above are true, you and your church desperately need revival. Chances are it must start with you and the born-again pastors of your community and then spread to the people. Ultimately, revival tarries until "your people, who are called by his name, humble themselves and pray." *Your* people.

Second Chronicles 7:14 is a marvelous blueprint for achieving a fresh work of God in your midst. If revival is to come, your people must:

- humble themselves.
- pray.
- turn from their wicked ways.

When these three things become a reality, God will:

- hear.
- forgive their sin.
- heal their church.

This familiar passage helps us understand the "engine" that drives revival, whether in Israel or the church, whether pastors or laymen, whether Pastoral Prayer Summits or church-wide Solemn Assemblies.

The goal of those entrusted with leadership is to discover and implement that which will revive, heal, and unite the genuine community of faith in common cause. This ancient text suggests that when we humble ourselves, he hears; when we pray, he forgives; when we turn, he heals our land.

In the case of Israel, God is talking about corporate culpability and corporate response. A community-wide response is the ideal. This would mean that pastors must keep an eye both on the condition of their own flock and that of the other fellowships in their community. Obviously, this would involve a change of thinking for many in pastoral leadership. "If my people . . . " says the Lord,

who dwell together in a twelve-tribe configuration;

who recognize Jerusalem as the theological center of their nation;

who live in geographically separated areas;

who face common enemies;

who were corporately delivered from Egypt;

If this group of people humble themselves and pray and turn from their wicked ways, God will move to heal the entire group. He will bring health, he will protect and provide for all of them, not just a select list of tribes. For us today, this suggests that Pastor X should pray for the revival of his church *and* the churches of the entire community.

But it's the old story. It starts with the leaders—and if you want people to bleed, you must hemorrhage.

Revival begins with shepherds, not sheep. That's what Pastoral Prayer Summits are all about. It's what separates Prayer Summits from other public prayer gatherings. It is highly unlikely that two or three hours of corporate prayer will accomplish what biblical models and our experience suggest must take several days in his presence, seeking his face.

Let me underscore that there is no "pat formula" for initiating revival. However, by looking at the way God has worked in the past, we can discern some of the key elements. The following eight phases are suggestive, not necessarily normative.

Phase One

Phase one is *revelation*. Revival often tarries because we lack a fresh vision of God and his redemptive purposes.

"I saw the LORD," writes Isaiah, "seated on a throne, high and exalted, and the train of his robe filled the temple" (Isaiah 6:1).

As the seraphs flew around the heavenly throne, they called out to one another

"Holy, holy, holy is the LORD Almighty;
the whole earth is full of his glory" (Isaiah 6:3).

The dynamism of his holiness was so great that at its very mention "the door-posts and thresholds shook and the temple was filled with smoke" (Isaiah 6:4). This awesome revelation of the glory of God bowled over the godly prophet Isaiah. A new and enlarged understanding of the grandeur and majesty of his holiness caused the prophet to cry out

Woe to me! . . . I am ruined! For I am a man of

unclean lips, and I live among a people of unclean
lips, and my eyes have seen the King, the LORD
Almighty (Isaiah 6:5).

Hold it right there! Isaiah, if you—one of the giants,
one of the greatest of the prophets—are a man of
unclean lips, what must we be?

True revival begins with the acknowledgment that
Isaiah is right; *we* are a people of unclean lips. That's
reality.

If we claim to be without sin, we deceive ourselves
and the truth is not in us (1 John 1:8).

Maturity is always a return to reality about ourselves.
The greatest strength of Prayer Summits are the hours of
uninterrupted praise and worship. Lives change in his
presence! The following comments from pastors underscore the importance of prolonged, uninterrupted time
with him.

We met with God; God met with us!

Over and over, hour after hour, the prayer, the
praise, and the celebration were beautiful, lifting,
faith building, and the cause for much joy in the
Lord.

After three days of praying, broken before him, I'm
ready to be used of him any way he wants.

When I came to the Summit I felt as if I had
become a piece of dry parchment, wrinkled and
crumpled up, ready to blow away. As I sat and
basked in the Presence of Jesus I began feeling like
a fresh bud on a fruit tree.

I like that: "a fresh bud on a fruit tree." That's
revival!

Phase Two

The second phase in this process of revival is *recognition*. Do we see the symptoms and recognize the wreckage? Or have we become complacent?

The psalmist saw the devastation. "I am like a desert owl, like an owl among the ruins" (Psalm 102:6)—and his heart is broken because of those ruins.

Folks, if the creeks are dry, the wells empty, the landscape devastated by insects and people are dying of the plague, it's time for action. If the enemy is flooding the land like a plague, the church cannot afford the luxury of prolonged theological reflection or exegetical interchange. It's a time for humility.

Look around you. Is something wrong? It might be us!

But we must not simply analyze a devastated cosmos or take our own spiritual pulses. It is not enough to catalog the satanic strongholds that have crept into the center of the church. Somehow our vision must go all the way to God and his eternal purposes for this tired old world.

Phase Three

"Broken before him" is more than a cliché. It happens. When we're dealing with God and he's dealing with us, fresh revelation prompts *repentance*. That's the third phase in the process that leads to revival. It takes great humility to repent, because none of us are repenters by nature. We don't "change our minds" easily, and that's what repentance is all about.

> "If my people, who are called by my name, will humble themselves and pray . . ." (2 Chronicles 7:14).

The self-knowledge we learn through prolonged prayer is humbling. Humility is being aware of our own moral weaknesses and being willing to turn to God in repentance. Humility is moral realism. It is one of the qualities that attracts the empowerment of God.

> God opposes the proud but gives grace to the humble (James 4:6).

> Humble yourselves, therefore, under God's mighty hand, that he may lift you up in due time (1 Peter 5:6).

The good news is that enablement (grace) and exaltation await those who are truly humbled before him. God looks for and blesses humility.

Humility is:

- moral realism. Seeing ourselves in the light of his holiness.
- esteeming others as better than ourselves.
- a quality that attracts the blessing of God.
- a willingness to turn to God in repentance.
- an attitude that rejoices in the success of others.
- the fruit of brokenness.
- freedom from having to win, to be "right."
- the foundation of unity.
- the mark of maturity. "Learn of me, for I am meek and lowly."
- the mark of authenticity.

All the great men and women of God I have known share this wonderful quality. It's a broken heart and a contrite spirit that captures the attention of our heavenly father. Humility seems to be the human foundation of and the basis for unity.

It's one thing to be broken; it's another to be contrite.

Brokenness and contrition are the children of time spent worshiping and praising God. They are the fruit of extended time in his glorious presence. At some time during a Prayer Summit, brokenness surfaces when:

- people are overcome with the holiness of God.
- the grace of God overwhelms the hearts of his people.
- the gap between preaching and practice seems insurmountable.
- problems seem unsolvable.
- barrenness becomes obvious.
- another's pain and hurt overwhelms those who enter into it.
- God's glorious presence overpowers.
- repentance is genuine.

One cannot help but be broken before him.

I remember being overcome, being broken by the awful wages of sin. We listened as a dear brother shared his abuse by his father, his addiction to pornography, and the consequences of that addiction. As he wept, we wept. Few could talk. Entering into his brokenness, we prayed for his deliverance and cleansing. And God answered our prayers.

One pastor writes:

What a mighty God is He! The God we worship took about forty of His flawed, imperfect servants and created a perfect environment.

A perfect environment? Yes, prolonged time worshiping, praising and adoring him eventually creates an environment where pastors—men of the cloth, the clergy, ministers—feel they can abandon their clerical role and just be people; an environment where they feel safe to admit parts of their struggle they have never made public; a setting where they can repent.

There are many unfinished agendas in life. It is not unusual for participants to reveal their need to be delivered from the tyranny of an abusive background. In these cases, they don't so much need repentance as release from the memory, the tyranny, the influence of a ravaged past.

I remember so well the evening when one pastor, with great emotion, poured out his hurt, his bewilderment, his sorrow at being the victim of his father's perversions. As he expressed his bitterness, another pastor walked up, sat down next to him and said, "I know exactly what you're facing—my dad abused me." Immediately, another pastor arose, joined the group and said, "It wasn't my dad, it was my uncle."

In another setting a dear pastor described how he was abused by both parents. His dad he could forgive, but his mother was another story. Surrounded by other wounded healers, undergirded by the presence of God, this pastor and others like him have experienced repentance and release.

God wants his people to pray through to humility and repentance. And why not? An unrepentant spirit is ultimately an expression of pride. And where pride reigns, unity is inevitably absent.

Phase Four

The fourth step in the process of revival is *renunciation* of sin. It is one thing to repent, it is quite another to renounce the sin as wicked, as inappropriate for one who is joined to Christ.

If we humble ourselves, pray, and *turn from our wicked ways*, God will act on our behalf. It's one thing to change my mind about something; it's a another to renounce it. Without renunciation, the process of repentance aborts.

Renunciation is like bending over a nail. It recognizes the loathsome nature of sin and its consequences. Renunciation also publicly declares its intent. Renunciation tests the genuineness of repentance.

Phase Five

Reconciliation is the fifth phase of the process leading to revival. Unfortunately, Christians are often long on repentance and short on reconciliation. Sin separates. The world's greatest problem is alienation; its greatest solution is reconcilation through Jesus Christ. Reconciliation is making things right again. It is moving from disunity to unity, estrangement to fellowship, enmity to resolution, indebtedness to "paid in full."

During one communion service, a pastor knelt beside me and whispered a request. His church had sinned against seven other churches represented at the Prayer Summit. Feeling a need for reconciliation, he asked if he could wash the feet of the pastors of those churches and personally ask their forgiveness. It was a wonderful time of healing of old wounds.

The desire for reconciliation grows naturally out of an environment in which meeting with God and seeking his agenda is all that matters. Big on God's list is that we "come to complete unity." Reconciliation is a major step toward unity. It needs to happen in communities all over America.

Phase Six

Restoration is the sixth stage leading to revival in the church. Restoration involves the recovery of spiritual stamina and the restoration of relationship. Certainly, the great shepherd "restores our soul." The psalmist reminds us that souls get sick and need the shepherd's touch. They become like a "piece of dry parchment." Even the souls of pastors. No less than our Great Shepherd invites all those who "labor and are heavy laden" to come to him, and he "will give them rest." People do labor and get weighed down by it all. Especially those in ministry.

Sometimes restoration takes place when prodigals come home.

Restoration of relationship should flow naturally from genuine repentance and renunciation. What a beautiful thing it is when brothers are reunited around the Lord.

This restoration can take place on many levels.

It can mean problems are resolved on a personal level.

It can mean different church families are reconciled.

It can mean denominational opposition and oppression is eliminated.

It can mean overcoming certain theological differences that have built unnecessary walls.

It can mean the local community of faith begins to restore the Body along the lines of John 17.

It may mean those who are estranged join together in common cause, with a mutual interest in each others' ministries.

Phase Seven

Restitution is the seventh phase in the process of revival. Sometimes our immaturity and our insular lives result in attitudes and actions that make restitution a necessity. It's one thing to repent; it's quite another to assume responsibility for damages.

Gossip, misrepresentation, unnecessary comments, and overt competition are all ways by which we undercut and destroy our brothers in the faith. Where appropriate, restitution is important. This can take place on an individual or corporate level.

One pastor discovered that a previous pastor had been treated very unfairly in the circumstances surrounding his severance. Because of his treatment, his wife and kids abandoned the things of the Lord. The pastor felt responsible to make this right and led his church to invite the family to a special service where not only repentance took place, but also financial restitution. It was entirely appropriate. Wonderfully, within a short period the family was restored in the Lord.

Phase Eight

Reconsecration is the eighth phase of the process of revival, the logical outcome of the other components. It's a fresh commitment to pursue that which is holy and pure. It can be a rededication to the person and work of God. In the Old Testament, they made and signed covenants that spelled out their intentions. I've seen pastors write out their vows of recommittal and share them with their peers. Communion can be a wonderful time of reconsecration.

While no two revivals are alike, they do share some common elements. These eight phases are to be considered in that light. If they are all present in a given situation, they may occur simultaneously or in a different order. As we have observed God working in dozens of Prayer Summits, these eight phases normally have been present.

The bottom line is that those who desire to see

revival fires burn must be committed to the long haul. As life unfolds before us, as we become "weary in well-doing," our souls, like dry parchment, will need a new revelation of God. Our proclivity to sin assures us there will be needed seasons of repentance. It is then that we must remember:

"If my people . . . "

9

SPIRITUAL DEFECTION: Its Symptoms, Causes, and Cure

There is no finish line," says Nike.

Nike is wrong. One divine puff and Israel's flame was out. An entire nation crossed one line too many, a divine "finish line," and God said, "I've had it, you're finished!"

They'd stoned one too many prophets, built one too many pagan temples, listened to one too many apostate priests, offered one too many sons on a pagan altar.

The defection was virtually complete. With few exceptions, everyone abandoned Yahweh and the temple in Jerusalem.

All twelve tribes defected. Both parts of the divided kingdom, Judah and Israel, became apostate. The priests and Levites became false shepherds. The kings built altars to pagan gods. It's no wonder God shut down the carnival.

Unhappily, spiritual defection is not an Old Testament phenomenon, a quirk of interest only to theologians and historians. Paul uses Israel's ancient defection as a warning for the church. In 1 Corinthians 10 he maintains that Israel's flame-outs are instructive for today. Spiritual decline is followed by judgment—a judgment which often results in the removal of God's presence and blessing.

The Cycle of Spiritual Decline

Israel had it all and lost it all. The people sinned corporately and were judged corporately. Ultimately, God divorced them. The armies of Assyria and Babylon were recruited to scatter them across a pagan landscape. God's city and temple went up in smoke, and the denizens of darkness carved another notch in their pistol grips.

The cycle of spiritual decline is no mystery. Alexander Fraser Tytler (1747-1813) wrote a book describing the fall of the Athenian Republic. He suggested that nations progress through the following sequence:

1. from bondage to spiritual faith;
2. from spiritual faith to great courage;
3. from courage to liberty;
4. from liberty to abundance;
5. from abundance to selfishness;
6. from selfishness to complacency;
7. from complacency to apathy;
8. from apathy to dependency;
9. from dependency back into bondage.

The cycle is chillingly familiar, the parallels obvious. God sent prophets to break the cycle, to return his wayward people to their God. Godly kings set up Solemn Assemblies to do business with God. Although Solemn Assemblies are congregation-focused and Prayer Summits are pastor-focused, they share many things in common. The goal of both is revival. They both demand extended periods of time. Sin is a central issue to both. Usually judgment is right around the corner if repentance is not quick and genuine.

The Old Testament records numerous revivals that grew out of Solemn Assemblies. The following list underscores these many calls to revival in the Old Testament.

1. *The Revival under Moses.* While the Summit at Sinai was transpiring between Moses and God, the Israelites were worshiping a golden calf (Exodus 32ff).

2. *The Revival under Samuel.* Eli's wicked sons had made a mockery out of the offerings unto the Lord. Temple worship had been desecrated. The Ark of the Covenant had been captured by the Philistines. (*See* 1 Samuel 7.)

3. *The Revival under David.* Following the corrupt reign of King Saul, David returned the Ark of the Covenant to the city of Jerusalem. A great revival was the result (1 Chronicles 15-16).

4. *The Revival under Asa.* Judah, filled with idolatry and the detestable practices of the surrounding nations, is called to repentance (2 Chronicles 14-16).

5. *The Revival under Jehoshaphat.* Attacked by Moab and Ammon, Jehoshaphat calls his nation to repentance (2 Chronicles 20).

6. *The Revival under Jehoiada.* Overcoming the wicked influence of Ahaziah, King of Judah, Jehoiada calls for national repentance and the restoration of temple worship (2 Chronicles 23).

7. *The Revival under Hezekiah.* Ahaz, Hezekiah's father, worshiped the gods of Damascus. Hezekiah calls both Israel and Judah to national repentance (2 Chronicles 29-30).

8. *The Revival under Josiah.* As a teenager, Josiah began to seek God. The rediscovery of the Law brought about a national revival (2 Chronicles 34-35).

9. *The Revival under Zerubbabel.* Following the completion of the temple, a great revival transpires (Ezra 6).

10. *The Revival under Ezra.* Ezra's brokenness before God resulted in a time of great repentance and restoration among the remnant in Jerusalem (Ezra 8-10).

11. *The Revival under Nehemiah.* Following the completion of the wall a great revival broke out. Ezra joined with other Levites in a prolonged time of the reading of the Law of Moses. This led to confession and rededication. Later, Nehemiah led another revival upon his return to Jerusalem (Nehemiah 8-13).

12. *The Revival under Joel.* Joel calls upon the priests to call a sacred assembly, to rend their hearts and not their garments (Joel 1-2).

In most cases, these Solemn Assemblies were necessary because of Israel's defection. From them we learn that God doesn't tolerate the wickedness of his covenant community, whether Israel or the Church. In fact, God allows himself to be taken captive rather than bless the efforts of ungodly leaders. He ordered Elijah to anoint not only the godly prophet Elisha, but the ungodly, pagan king of Syria—a king who later brought grief to apostate Israel.

Israel's apostasy also instructs us that when believers are unfaithful, God unleashes the enemy. In effect, he calls in artillery upon himself. The psalmist writes:

> They burned your sanctuary to the ground; they defiled the dwelling place of your Name. They said in their hearts, "We will crush them completely!" They burned every place where God was worshiped in the land (Psalm 74:7-8).

No wonder the psalmist cried out, "How long will the enemy mock you, O God?" (v. 10).

The Place of Solemn Assemblies

Israel's cyclic pilgrimage highlights God's involvement in bringing about revival. Yes, the enemies of God mocked and they burned, pillaged and defiled. For a season they prevailed. And for a season, God stood back and let it happen, waiting for his people to "throw in the towel." When it finally hit the mat, God delivered. Genuine repentance unleashed the power of God on numerous occasions. It still does.

Dying, troubled, stagnant churches probably need to call a Solemn Assembly and face the reality of their defection. It's not a novel or new idea. Churches did it in other centuries. The model of Israel's cyclic spirituality has great potential for the Church today.

Solemn Assemblies were necessary to break Israel's cycles of spiritual defection. To defect means to abandon and to embrace. Defectors abandon one set of loyalties to embrace another. It is not unusual for churches to abandon . . .

the grace of God and embrace legalism.
evangelism and embrace universalism.
the Word and embrace secular humanism.
the Lordship of Christ and embrace human potential.
the Spirit and embrace human effort and achievement.
the Body and embrace sectarianism.
unity and embrace denominationalism.
the lost world and embrace a selfish agenda.
the "one way" of Scripture and embrace "many ways."
purity and embrace sensuality.
biblical miracles and embrace scientism.
cooperation and embrace competition.
God and embrace themselves.

Paul's Autopsy on Ancient Israel

All such defection moves one further away from the blessing of God and closer to the judgment of God. Paul's autopsy of Israel gives us insight into the dynamics of spiritual decline and how to avoid it. Could it be that the Spirit directed Paul to record an analysis of Israel's decline and fall so that the Church could avoid its errors?

It's true that if we ignore the lessons of history we are destined to repeat them. Spiritual defection is no mystery. It should be noted that the apostle is using the experience of ancient Israel to warn the church at Corinth against exactly this kind of defection. It is not just an Old Testament phenomenon. The divine etiology of spiritual decline is highly instructive.

Paul's tracing of such a spiritual heritage reminds us that a nation, denomination, or church, like Israel, can "have it all" and still be a candidate for serious apostasy. In chapter ten of his first epistle to the Corinthians, Paul takes the first four verses to profile four distinct spiritual advantages that Israel enjoyed.

1. They had daily, divine direction: they "were all under the cloud" (v. 1). The cloud and pillar of fire kept them in the place of God's choice.

2. They had all experienced a mighty deliverance: "they all passed through the sea" (v. 1). What a phenomenal demonstration of the saving power of their God!

3. They had an extraordinary leader: "they were all baptized into Moses" (v. 2). It was under his leadership that they were delivered from Egypt, crossed the Red Sea, received the law, the tabernacle, and numerous deliverances from danger. No leader since has excelled Moses in ability or character. They had a wonderful "pastor."

4. They shared a rich spiritual diet: "they all ate the same spiritual food and drank the same spiritual drink; . . . from the spiritual rock . . . and that rock was Christ" (v. 3-4).

It doesn't get any better than that. They had a wonderful spiritual heritage. But the result?

God was not pleased with most of them; their bodies were scattered over the desert (v. 5).

Paul brings the ancient defection of Israel right up to the present when he declares,

Now these things occurred as examples, to keep us from setting our hearts on evil things . . .

These things . . . were written down as warnings for us, on whom the fulfillment of the ages has come (vs. 6,11).

Israel's history, Paul reminds us, is not to be stored in some dusty tome; it is a classic case study of how well-informed people turn from the true God and abort their divine commission. The process is like a slow leak, not a blowout.

As a general rule, there is no outward evidence of spiritual decline at the beginning. According to Paul, defection begins with the inclination of the heart. We are not to "set our hearts on evil things as they did" (1 Corinthians 10:6). But God's chosen, much blessed people do set their hearts on evil things.

Sure, they attend all the services, say the right things, put their tithes in the offering plate, and pray at the proper time. But their hearts aren't in it. Other values creep into their minds. Other options for living crowd out the narrow strictures of their faith. Though on the surface all appears well, a subtle process is at work. And when the core values begin to change, it's not long before the defection begins to surface.

Ultimately, our actions are controlled by our dominant thoughts.

If I sow a thought,
  I'll reap an act.
If I sow an act,
  I'll reap a habit.
If I sow a habit,
  I'll reap a character.
If I sow a character,
  I'll reap a destiny.

If in the secret recesses of my mind I mull over that which is wrong, fantasize over evil, a day will come when that which populates the theater of my mind becomes reality. Satan will see to that! That is why we are to bring all thoughts into captivity to Christ.

Harbored long enough, a thought becomes an act, a part of my history. But I'm not alone. As others' fantasies break through the surface and also become visible, as they "come out of the closet," they reinforce those whose minds are harboring similar ideas. And like an infection, the contagion spreads throughout the entire population. It is then that the storm clouds of judgment begin to build!

For reasons like this, Solomon wrote, "Above all else, guard your heart, for it is the wellspring of life." "Cursed is the one," writes Jeremiah, "who trusts in man, who depends on flesh for his strength and whose heart turns away from the LORD" (Jeremiah 17:5). "Cursed" means "headed for trouble."

An Ancient Pathology Report

Having established that the root of apostasy is the inclination of the heart, Paul cuts deeper into the corpse of ancient Israel. He does this so that the church can learn from Israel's pathology report. He cites four reasons for her decline and death.

1. The first stage of spiritual defection is idolatry. "Do not," writes Dr. Paul, "be idolaters, as some of them were" (1 Corinthians 10:7). When my heart is inclined toward anything other than the agenda of God, I am an idolater. An idol is that which has captured some of the devotion owed only to Almighty God. It can be:

a person,
a career,
a ministry,
a hobby,
a possession,
an obsession,
a habit,
a position,
a creed,
a denomination,
a doctrinal statement.

At its very root, *idolatry is a demonic strategy to give an individual permission to indulge in his strongest natural desires without guilt.* As the inclination of the heart moves toward that which is evil, a moral crisis begins to develop. That flashing red light starts to spoil the fulfillment of those perverted inclinations. Israel's spiritual heritage collided with the carnal inclination of her heart.

In such circumstances, something has to give. So what gives?

At Horeb [Sinai] they made a calf and worshiped an idol cast from metal.

They exchanged their Glory for an image of a bull, which eats grass.

They forgot the God who saved them, who had done great things in Egypt, miracles in the land of Ham and awesome deeds by the Red Sea (Psalm 106:19-22).

Notice the verbs: *They made, worshiped, exchanged, and forgot.*

What did they do to free themselves to indulge in their strongest natural desires? They redefined God. They traded in their God of Glory for the image of a grass-chewing bull.

"God? Oh, don't worry about him. He's out in the pasture. We'll toss him a bale of hay. He'll be just fine."

How did the Greeks justify ten thousand temple prostitutes in Corinth? Quite simple. They bought into the lie of an adulterous pantheon of gods who were themselves promiscuous. Wouldn't you feel better indulging in your strongest natural desire if your god was a champion of your inclination? The ultimate fantasy would be to link that indulgence with religion, with a deity who promoted your pet sin as a legitimate expression of worship. Ever wonder why so many current religious cults have sexual freedom as one of their cardinal doctrines?

Self-preservation is another strong natural desire. It can quickly be transformed into selfishness and self-centeredness, a "me first" mentality. To put "me first" is idolatry. True worship is "your kingdom come, your will be done." A sensual or self-centered heart is often the first step toward defection.

2. *The second stage of spiritual defection is immorality.* Does it surprise you that Paul lists immorality as the next component of spiritual defection? It shouldn't.

Immorality describes that which is not moral, that which is immoral. It can refer to many things.

- Charging too much for rent is immoral.
- Ignoring the homeless is immoral.
- Partaking of communion in an unworthy manner is immoral.
- Cheating is immoral.
- Putting ministry ahead of family can be immoral.
- Cruelty and abuse is immoral.
- Profiting from religion is immoral.
- Taking advantage of the weaknesses of others is immoral.
- Viewing pornography is immoral.
- Dividing the body is immoral.

So is illicit sex. And that's what Paul talks about as the second stage of Israel's defection. "We should not commit sexual immorality, as some of them did—and in one day twenty-three thousand of them died" (1 Corinthians 10:8). Paul isn't suggesting that everyone who defects has been unfaithful. Some type of immorality, however, seems to be a component part of most spiritual defection.

At nearly every Prayer Summit some pastor or Christian leader confesses his addiction to pornography. It is not unusual for several to repent of this sin and seek forgiveness and deliverance. What a joy it has been to see God bring healing!

Who can imagine how much division and discord is caused by church leaders, elders, and deacons who are secretly addicted to some type of sexual perversion? One cannot imagine the guilt they must feel. The tragedy is that the congregation pays for their secret sins.

Just recently I heard the story of a pastor who was

called to a church with serious spiritual problems. Somehow the blessing and presence of God seemed absent. Laboring in prayer over this issue, the pastor had a vision. In the vision he was in the sanctuary in front of the communion table lifting up the furnace grate and reaching under it for something. Curious, he went to the sanctuary, lifted the grate and reached down under the floorboards under the communion table, and discovered a cache of pornographic magazines. He confessed the sins of his predecessor and God restored his presence and blessing to this church.

3. *The third phase of spiritual defection is insubordination.* At this stage in the defection process, the individual has broken two solemn covenants. He has broken his covenant with God through his idolatry and is thus a spiritual prostitute. Second, he has broken a covenant with his mate and has thus prostituted his marriage or his sexuality. He's in serious trouble and faces an important decision point. He either repents of all that has transpired, or he blames God.

We should not test the Lord, as some of them did—
and were killed by snakes (1 Corinthians 10:9).

"God, you brought us out into this wilderness to kill us and our children! It's your fault. Everything would be OK if you'd only left us alone in Egypt!"

Though it cost me about $100 to fix the thing, it was OK that my son turned the spark plugs the wrong way and ruined the head of my outboard motor. It was not OK when he said, "Dad, if you wouldn't have suggested I check the plugs, this would not have happened."

It's called rationalization.

"If only you'd made me handsome."

"If only you'd given me the gifts of Chuck Swindoll."

"If only you'd hidden that *Playboy* from me."

"If only you'd given me a more significant ministry."

"If only you'd not given me such a strong sex drive."

"If only you'd not given me such a sorry board."

"If only you'd provide more money for my needs."

"If only you'd left me alone."

"If only you'd given me a larger congregation."

"If only you'd get me out of the inner city."

"It's your fault, Lord, that nothing's happening."

God sent snakes to take care of people who blamed him for their sin. Rationalization precludes repentance and restoration.

4. The fourth phase of spiritual defection is impudence. Impudent children can be cute. Can't you just see that turned-up nose, the clenched fists, the "don't you touch me" stance, that cynical tone of voice?

Impudent adults stink. Paul says, "Do not grumble, as some of them did—and were killed by the destroying angel" (10:10).

We're talking about a jaded, cynical attitude toward the things of God and life itself. Churches are full of people who have lost the joy, who are professional skeptics, who sow seeds of discord. It usually takes two to grumble, the grumbler and the grumblee. These sorry creatures are down on everything. Pessimistic and negative, they douse faith and vision. In reality, they grumble against the very plan and purpose of God. It is no wonder such people were killed by "the destroying angel."

Turning from Israel on the operating table, Paul faces you and me and says, "Let him who thinks he stands take heed lest he fall." When a church is full of idolaters, those who are immoral, stubborn, and cynical, the only cure may be radical . . . a Solemn Assembly.

Sometimes spiritual log-jams can only be broken up by inducing a crisis; by taking strong measures to confront sin and apostasy.

Because Solemn Assemblies and Prayer Summits are cousins, they share many dynamics in common. Perhaps a closer examination of the Solemn Assembly will further our understanding of a Prayer Summit.

10.

SPIRITUAL CRISIS MANAGEMENT: An Old Testament Blueprint

Did you want to kill him, Buck?"

"Well, I bet I did."

"What did he do to you?"

"Him? He never done nothing to me."

"Well, then, what did you want to kill him for?"

"Why, nothing—only it's on account of the feud."

"What's a feud?"

"Why, where was you raised? Don't you know what a feud is?"

"Never heard of it before—tell me about it."

"Well," says Buck, "a feud is this way: A man has a quarrel with another man and kills him; then that other man's brother kills him; then the other brothers, on both sides, goes for one another; then the cousins chip in—and by and by everybody's killed off, and there ain't no more feud. But it's kind of slow, and takes a long time."

"Has this been going on long, Buck?"

"Well, I should reckon! It started thirty years ago, or som'ers along there. There was trouble 'bout something, and then a law-suit to settle it; and the suit went agin one of the men, and so he up and shot the man that won the suit—which he would naturally do, of course. Anybody would."

"What was the trouble about, Buck?—land?"

"I reckon maybe—I don't know."

"Well, who done the shooting? Was it a Grangerford or a Shepherdson?"

"Laws, how do I know? It was so long ago."

"Don't anybody know?"

"Oh, yes, pa knows, I reckon, and some of the other old people; but they don't know now what the row was about in the first place."

Mark Twain,
The Adventures of Huckleberry Finn

It's highly doubtful Israel and Judah knew what their row was about either! For sure they didn't understand the spiritual roots of their civil war. After generations of hassle, Yahweh pulled up his glory and went home.

And why shouldn't he? His feuding followers wouldn't listen to the judges or the prophets.

After several "silent centuries," God once again threw his glove in the ring and made his comeback. Angelic choirs backed up the glory of the Lord as it splashed all over the Bethlehem landscape, startling the tar out of some sleepy shepherds. The manger-born redeemer returned to tag another group of people as the new address for his name, a "habitation of God through the Spirit."

His indwelling is really a double-dip deal. He indwells the individual believer whose body becomes his temple. Likewise, he indwells the Church as a temple built of living stones. "Living stones" may well be a euphemism. Alive? Yes. All those who are born anew are alive in Christ. Living? That's another question.

Once again, God takes the risk of linking his reputation to that of his followers. "By this," the Lord reminds us, "all men will know that you are my disciples, if you love one another."

As members of the second incarnation, believers have the responsibility to make visible the invisible God in the same way Christ did. It's a wonderful strategy, but not a fool-proof one. The first-century church was plagued with problems that continue to this day.

Learning from the First-Century Church

"You have forsaken your first love."

"You have people there who hold to the teaching of Balaam . . . [and] the Nicolaitans."

"You tolerate that woman Jezebel."

"You have a reputation of being alive, but you are dead."

"You are neither cold nor hot . . ." (Revelation 2-3).

The charges brought against the seven churches of Asia Minor include:

- Alienation of affection.
- Doctrinal deviation.
- Immorality.
- Sterility.
- Complacency.

Six times these letters call the churches of Asia Minor to repent. The whole congregation—everyone— is called upon to repent.

Though unfamiliar to this generation, corporate repentance was a vital part of church life in America in its early days. Harvard's Weidener Library contains a significant number of sermons preached at just such Solemn Assemblies. Our American forefathers in the faith took sin and repentance seriously.

How should we respond when we see churches caught up in the same sins? What should church leaders do when they feel "the glory of God has departed"?

The Old Testament Solemn Assembly

The Old Testament Solemn Assembly provides an excellent model for such repentance. Though the dozen or so revivals in the Old Testament differ in details, they share some common threads.

1. Spiritual defection precedes the Solemn Assembly.

Paul warned Corinthian believers against idolatry, immorality, insubordination, and impudence. In most cases, it is this moral and spiritual decline that makes revival a necessity. A church needing to proclaim a Solemn Assembly is one where:

there is a leadership crisis.

there is a divided congregation.

there is doctrinal defection.

there is impurity and immorality.

there is disunity and disharmony.

there is no growth.

there is no vision.

there are unresolved problems.

there is an unwillingness to be reconciled.

there is a lukewarm congregation.

there is a history of divisiveness.

there is no glory.

Certainly the Lord of the Church has moved through it and removed the candlesticks of many congregations. He removes the glory of his presence even though they continue to meet, take offerings, and play church. I remember as a young man Dr. T. J. Bach told me, "Never minister in a church where the glory of God has departed."

2. *Most Old Testament revivals have been preceded by divine judgment.*

It shouldn't surprise us that the Lord of the church is described as moving in judgment against moral and spiritual decline in his church. Listen to his warnings in Revelation 2 and 3.

> "If you do not repent, I will come to you and remove your lampstand from its place."

> "Repent, therefore! Otherwise, I will soon come to you and will fight against them with the sword of my mouth."

> "I will strike her children dead. Then all the churches will know that I am he who searches hearts and minds, and I will repay each of you according to your deeds."

> "Wake up! Strengthen what remains and is about to die, for I have not found your deeds complete in the sight of my God."

> "If you do not wake up, I will come like a thief . . ."

Wake up! God's wake-up call is often judgment. The Old Testament documents several divine judgments that resulted in death and destruction. But not all judgments were final and fatal. Sometimes the very fact that God marched an army against his people drove them to their knees in prayer and repentance. Famine was another way he got their attention. The prophet Joel writes:

> Has not the food been cut off before our very eyes

... The seeds are shriveled beneath the clods ...
The herds mill about because they have no pasture; even the flocks of sheep are suffering (Joel 1:16-18).

"I gave you empty stomachs in every city and lack of bread in every town, yet you have not returned to me," declares the LORD (Amos 4:6).

When Israel was in a time of spiritual decline, God often withdrew his presence from her, refusing to listen to her prayers. Sometimes he declared that even if she sought him, he would not be found. Isaiah writes:

But your iniquities have separated you from your God; your sins have hidden his face from you, so that he will not hear (Isaiah 59:2).

Furthermore, he anointed pagan kings to come up against her.

Quarreling, impurity, disunity, church splits, interdenominational strife, and doctrinal deviation preclude the blessing of God. Paul labels such responses as carnal and childish.

3. *Most Old Testament revivals originated in the heart of a godly, brokenhearted leader.*

Nehemiah's response to the condition of Jerusalem is instructive.

When I heard these things, I sat down and wept. For some days I mourned and fasted and prayed before the God of heaven (Nehemiah 1:4).

When the long-forgotten Book of the Law was discovered in the temple it was brought to Josiah the king. "When the king heard the words of the Law, he tore his robes" (2 Chronicles 34:19).

When word came to Ezra that Israelites, including priests and Levites, had intermarried with their pagan neighbors, he "tore [his] tunic and cloak, pulled hair from [his] head and beard and sat down appalled" (Ezra 9:3). Falling on his knees with his hands spread out to the Lord, Ezra prayed:

> O my God, I am too ashamed and disgraced to lift up my face to you, my God, because our sins are higher than our heads and our guilt has reached to the heavens. . . .

> Because of our sins, we and our kings and our priests have been subjected to the sword and captivity, to pillage and humiliation at the hand of foreign kings, as it is today (Ezra 9:6-7).

In the same way, nothing less than a broken heart can overcome the spiritual inertia of a disobedient, complacent church.

> The LORD is close to the brokenhearted and saves those who are crushed in spirit (Psalm 34:18).

> The sacrifices of God are a broken spirit; a broken and contrite heart, O God, you will not despise (Psalm 51:17).

4. Most Old Testament revivals were kindled by men who took sin seriously.

These leaders recognized that God's judgment upon them was the result of unconfessed corporate sin. Let me say it again. Perceptive spiritual leadership recognizes that the lack of blessing, the lack of the presence of the Lord, the lack of growth, is usually the result of unconfessed corporate sin.

The Lord of the Church declared, "I will build my

church, and the gates of Hades will not overcome it." To the Acts 2 church he "added to their number daily those who were being saved."

And yet most of American Christendom knows nothing of such growth.

What's the Problem?

What's wrong today? Why are 80 percent of the churches in the United States not growing? Could it be that all across America spiritual leaders need to be shaken, need to assume responsibility for their churches, and call a time for confession and repentance? Do they need to foster the truth of a corporate church in their community composed of believers outside their immediate fellowship?

If a church is not reaching the lost, shouldn't that be repented of?

If a church is divided and full of strife, shouldn't that be repented of?

If a church has a history of splits and divisions, shouldn't that be repented of?

If a church has been unfair in its treatment of its pastoral staff, shouldn't that be repented of?

If a church has not maintained purity, shouldn't that be repented of?

If a church has been critical of other Bible-believing churches, shouldn't that be repented of?

If a church has compromised biblical theology, shouldn't that be repented of?

If a church has no concern for the poor and downtrodden, shouldn't that be repented of?

If a church's worship is cold, formal, and lacks life, shouldn't that be repented of?

If a church has made its traditions sacred, shouldn't that be repented of?

If a church board is divided, shouldn't that be repented of?

If a church is overcome with materialism, shouldn't that be repented of?

If a church has no vision for world missions, shouldn't that be repented of?

If a church has been guilty of racial and ethnic prejudice, shouldn't that be repented of?

If a church is lukewarm for God, shouldn't that be repented of?

The lists goes on and on.

Almost inevitably, a dying church has a history of disunity, splits, immorality, pretense, legalism, complacency, disobedience, and lack of vision. No such church should expect the blessing of God without corporate confession of sin. He does not pour out his blessing indiscriminately.

The same Satan who "rose up against Israel" has risen up against the church (1 Chronicles 21:1). He who divided Israel is dividing the church. Is it any wonder the Lord prayed that we might be one?

Many churches don't want to grow. Some have leaders who delight in running off pastors. Others treat their pastors like dogs. There are churches "owned" by laymen. Many are overcome with legalism and a judgmental spirit. Kingdom-building pastors ruin not a few churches.

And we wonder why few churches in America are growing? The issue isn't money or facilities or location. Ultimately, the church needs a responsible, biblical way to induce a crisis of sufficient magnitude to break it loose from whatever may be holding it back. Most of all, it needs leaders who will courageously call it back to its mission.

Old Testament Revivalists

The successful Old Testament revivalists were full participants in corporate confession and repentance. They refused to blame others. They not only shouldered the burden of a disobedient, complacent, idolatrous congregation, they confessed their own failures.

Moses fasted and prayed for forty days.

Nehemiah wept and prayed.

Jehoshaphat proclaimed a fast for all Judah.

God told Josiah "Because your heart was responsive and you . . . humbled yourself before me and tore your robes and wept in my presence, I have heard you . . ." (2 Chronicles 34:27).

Ezra said, "Here we are before you in our guilt, though because of it not one of us can stand in your presence" (Ezra 9:15).

These leaders called sin sin. They accepted responsibility for the defection of their people. They didn't pass the buck or blame a previous leader. It was not unusual for them to confess their own sins.

While Ezra was praying and confessing, weeping and throwing himself down before the house of God, a large crowd of Israelites . . . gathered around him. They too wept bitterly (Ezra 10:1).

Nehemiah said:

I confess the sins we Israelites, including myself and my father's house, have committed against you. We have acted very wickedly toward you. We have not obeyed the commands, decrees and laws you gave your servant Moses (Nehemiah 1:6-7).

Isaiah wrote:

For our offenses are many in your sight, and our sins testify against us (Isaiah 59:12).

Daniel prays:

O Lord . . . we have sinned and done wrong. We have been wicked and have rebelled; we have turned away from your commands and laws.

O Lord, we . . . are covered with shame because we have sinned against you (Daniel 9:4,5,8).

Notice how Daniel owned up to the issue of sin. The angel Gabriel came to him, he records,

While I was speaking and praying, confessing my sin and the sin of my people Israel . . . (Daniel 9:20).

It is not unusual for pastors to return from a Prayer Summit and the next Sunday confess their fears, their shortcomings, their lack of faith, their lack of vision to their own people. Significant changes have taken place as a result.

Humility of heart captures the attention of God. In fact, his eyes "move to and fro throughout the whole earth to show himself strong on behalf of those whose hearts are right before him."

If God's people will humble themselves and pray, if they will seek God's face and turn from their wickedness, "then will I hear from heaven," says God, "and will forgive their sin and will heal their land" (2 Chronicles 7:14).

5. *Old Testament Solemn Assemblies involved individual and corporate confession, repentance, reconciliation and restoration.*

God calls Israel to:

"Return to me with all your heart, with fasting and weeping and mourning." Rend your heart and not your garments (Joel 2:12-13).

Rid yourselves of all the offenses you have committed, and get a new heart and a new spirit (Ezekiel 18:31).

Confession presupposes awareness of sin. In times of spiritual defection it is the responsibility of leadership to discover those individual and corporate sins that have brought judgment against the church and then confront them in a biblical manner. This may well involve an inventory of the "sins of the church fathers." Unreconciled problems from the past siphon off spiritual power.

We've already noted that "during the reign of David there was a famine for three successive years" (see 2 Samuel 21:1). As you could well imagine, David sought the face of the Lord. The Lord said, "It is on account of Saul and his blood-stained house; it is because he put the Gibeonites to death" (2 Samuel 21:1).

David's nation underwent judgment for the disobedience of a former, now dead, king. Furthermore, wasn't the treaty made with the Gibeonites consummated over four hundred years before David's rule? And hadn't the Gibeonites deceived Israel with their "worn-out" clothes and "tired" food?

You mean to say that God would bring three years of famine into a congregation because of the sins of previous leadership? "Pastor" David experienced famine because "Pastor" Saul was disobedient? Could the deadness, the lack of vitality in your church be the result of the "sins of the fathers"? Are they passed on?

In David's case they were. And it took the deaths of Saul's seven sons to remedy the situation. "After that, God answered prayer in behalf of the land" (2 Samuel 21:14).

6. *Old Testament Solemn Assemblies were often prolonged and intense.*

Sometimes days were spent in mourning and fasting. They were not a time for business as usual. Honeymoons were cut short, women and children were required to be present. Even nursing mothers were not exempt.

While in the pastorate, I concluded that the average elder/deacon had probably never spent more than an hour or so in genuine prayer with his fellow leaders. But an hour of prayer only begins to "clear out the cobwebs." Naively I suggested we get away overnight for extended prayer and worship. Our only agenda was to be in the presence of God for an extended period of time. All church business was left behind. God knit our hearts together and fused us into a unified team. I point to these prolonged times in his presence as the single greatest factor in our rapid growth.

I believe God used our elder-board summits as a model for starting Prayer Summits for pastors. While a Solemn Assembly focuses on the corporate body—Israel or the Church—the Prayer Summit focuses on leadership. While the goal of the Prayer Summit is personal renewal, the goal of the Solemn Assembly is corporate renewal. The two events share much in common, yet they are different.

In the next chapter I will give some specific suggestions for setting up a Solemn Assembly, and in the chapters following we'll refocus on the Prayer Summit.

11.
THE SOLEMN ASSEMBLY IN THE LOCAL CHURCH: Nursing the Body Back to Health

I was brought up on Solemn Assemblies.

My father and I had more Solemn Assemblies than I care to remember. These existential encounters typically took place in the basement. As I recall, things got real solemn on the way down the basement stairs. In that environment, even my marvelous sense of humor didn't help much. Dad pretty well controlled the agenda!

Generally, the trip to the basement was solemn because all recourse or due process had expired. Promises like, "I'll never do it again" were of no avail. "I'm sorry, I'm sorry, I'm sorry" didn't seem to help much, either.

For the most part, the solemnity of the occasion was due to the behavior and attitudes that preceded this bonding experience. In fact, there seemed to be a direct correlation between the seriousness of the offense and the solemnity of the occasion. It was almost as though there was a Richter Scale. The 3.4s were survivable, but look out for the 6.8s.

Inducing a Crisis in the Church

When things aren't going well, when sin abounds, when discipline is long overdue, sometimes it's necessary to induce a crisis in the relationship to help the wayward start building momentum in the right direction. I'm told that during the Welsh Revival if a church went two years without an obvious move of God in their midst, they would call a Solemn Assembly and seek God.

Jehoshaphat called a Solemn Assembly because the enemy was hotfooting it his way. Hezekiah called for a Solemn Assembly because the priesthood was corrupt and the nation divided. In Josiah's case, it was the rediscovery of the Law, God's Word, that proved to be the catalyst for revival. Joel exhorts the priests to call a Solemn Assembly and to rend their hearts, not their garments.

Of course, these examples are all Old Testament. Some would conclude, therefore, that these solemn occasions are not for today. That's an unfortunate conclusion. Many churches across the country are ripe for a Solemn Assembly, a time when they set aside the routine and deal with reality.

In the Old Testament, the Solemn Assembly was targeted on Joe-citizen, not upon Joseph-the-priest. Everyone was expected to attend. Wives and children were to be there. Honeymooners were expected to show up. It was not a time for business as usual. Sometimes these assemblies lasted for days.

The word "solemn" underscores the seriousness of the occasion and the gravity of the situation. We should get solemn:

when we realize we're in over our heads.

when the "glory of God" has departed from our churches.

where sin abounds.

when church leaders are in disarray.

when no one is coming to Christ.

when worship is dead.

when there is no vision.

when the Word falls on deaf ears.

when carnality prevails.

when sin is condoned.

when unity is AWOL.

when the perimeters of control are out of control.

where effective individual and corporate prayer is weak or nonexistent.

where a spirit of criticism prevails.

Do you get the picture? So how do we respond to a stagnant ministry?

Suggested Guidelines for a Solemn Assembly

The following items are suggestions and must be adapted to each situation. Perhaps they will stimulate your thinking along the lines of what would be most effective for your church.

1. Start at the top.

An organization is simply the shadow of its leader cast long. If you're the pastor or a church leader, find some time alone with God. There are no "quick fixes." I suggest you participate in a Pastoral Prayer Summit. Not only would you experience the wonderful restoration of your soul, but you'd no longer need to minister in isolation. You would have some brothers and sisters who would support you and your dreams and hold you accountable. Remember, maturity is always a return to reality about yourself!

2. Take your leadership team away on a mini-Prayer Summit.

A Friday night-Saturday schedule works just fine.

When I pastored, we did this regularly. Leave behind your file folders, business items, and other agendas. The only agenda is to seek the face of God.

It's time to pray, not talk about the need for it.

It's a time to worship, not to talk about it.

It's a time for individual and corporate examination.

It's a time for team-building.

Quite likely:

It's a time for repentance and reconciliation. Leaders must become one before they attempt to promote unity.

It's a time to hear the voice of God and covenant together to face whatever is necessary to see the restoration of God's blessing.

It's a time to identify and catalogue the sins of the church.

It's a time to determine the magnitude of the problem.

It's a time to prayerfully consider the implications of the John 17 model.

To neglect a careful analysis of the spiritual climate of the church is to invite the judgment of God. In 1 Corinthians 11 Paul makes it clear that people are diminished individually and corporately, physically and spiritually, if they enter into worship (specifically communion) with unresolved sin in their lives.

Our Lord suggested forgoing participation in worship until one is reconciled to an offended brother. Paul calls each believer to "examine himself" to ascertain readiness to share in communion. It took the temple cleaners sixteen days to rid the temple of junk and prepare it for the reinstitution of worship that was pleasing to God.

In Revelation 2-3 the Lord commends and warns the corporate Church and, where necessary, calls them to repentance. That's the job of leadership. An actual inventory of sin can be a catalyst to repentance. As leaders pray over the church and invite God to search its corporate heart, sins of all kinds will undoubtedly surface.

As the leaders wait before the Lord, appoint someone to jot down the transgressions that surface. In this exercise you are cataloging both individual and corporate sins. It is not a time to sit around with eyes open and brainstorm. Nor is it a witch hunt.

Undoubtedly, some of the problems will involve the board itself and its leadership (or lack of it). Let the data be generated out of prayer, out of talking with God about those things that break his heart or offend his holiness. It is a time of prayer in which person after person talks to God about what the Spirit brings to mind.

"Lord, we have been divided as a board."

"Father, our worship has become cold."

"We have lost our vision."

"Dear God, we've been a source of division in the body."

"Father, we have not maintained the purity of our church."

"We have a history of splits."

"We have failed to exercise church discipline."

"We have failed to deal with the sins of our fathers."

"We have allowed satanic strongholds to exist at the heart of the church."

The list could consist of such items as:

- disunity
- gossip
- dissension
- immorality
- lack of church discipline
- stinginess
- critical spirits
- no vision
- hatred
- perversion

- the sins of the church fathers
- sins against former leaders
- greed
- indifference
- cynicism
- selfishness
- disobedience
- substance abuse
- legalism
- spiritual apathy
- lying
- hypocrisy

Very likely the list will include sinful actions as well as attitudes, sins of commission as well as omission.

The naming and recording of these trespasses will break your heart. After a season of prayer have someone read the list . . . and repent. Leaders need to do it. They must set the pace. Nehemiah did, Hezekiah did, Ezra did, and Daniel did. You must, too.

3. Secure reconciliation between church leaders.

It is to be hoped that the leadership Prayer Summit will facilitate any necessary repentance and reconciliation. Let a time of communion solidify their commitment to God and to each other. In our Pastor's Prayer Summits we make a big point about not taking communion unless things are right with God and man. Be bold enough to ask if there are things that need to be made right between leaders. An unfinished agenda at this point can and will abort the process.

4. Obtain a leadership covenant to act.

It is critical that before a crisis is induced in the church, leadership support the decision to schedule a Solemn Assembly and agree upon the process to achieve its goals. I suggest that a written agreement be drawn up that spells out the actions to be taken to bring about a revival in the church. Each leader should sign the document and support it. The idea of a Solemn Assembly may be challenged by church members. The board must stand as one in its support of it.

5. Before publicly announcing the Solemn Assembly, have the leadership team meet weekly for extended times of prayer.

This allows the covenant agreement to season. It will also solidify the leaders in their commitment to each other and to the process. Furthermore, it will open their eyes to the true condition of the church.

6. Determine the dates for such an occasion.

As we shall see, a Solemn Assembly is both an event and a process that leads up to a climactic event. If the church calendar is busy, clear it so that you will have a window of several weeks to focus on repentance and renewal.

7. Announce the process to the church.

It is important to have leaders visually present when the announcement is made. It should be a solemn announcement that sends a signal that it is not business as usual. The announcement should include explanations that include why, when, where, how, and who.

Without going into great detail, the "why" part of the explanation should include a summary of the sins and failures identified at the leadership Prayer Summit. Have an elder or deacon read the list of sins identified by the leaders. The very act of reading the list informs the congregation of the seriousness of the situation and the board's intent to deal with it. At this point it would probably be good to list categories of sins, rather than failures that could focus on a particular individual or event. The items might include statements like these:

"We have allowed a divisive spirit to pervade the church."

"Our church has lost its zeal for evangelism."

"We are not seeing people come to faith in Christ."

"We have allowed impurity to dwell in our midst."

"Leadership has been divided."

"We have been a legalistic community."

"Our fellowship has publicly spoken against other evangelical ministries."

"We have lost our zeal for a lost world."

"Materialism and secularism have crept into our fellowship."

"We have neglected to choose leaders who meet the biblical qualifications."

"We are a prayerless people."

"We lack vision, we're drifting."

"We have a history of running off pastors."

"We have not been faithful in seeking reconciliation."

The "when" part should also be explained. Probably a five- to six-week period should be established, with the Solemn Assembly being the climactic event. The duration of the process is to be determined by the seriousness of the problem.

The "how" dimension should also be included. The process will call for preaching that focuses on revival; special prayer meetings; times for personal reflection climaxed by the Assembly itself. If necessary, the normal weekly schedules may be altered to allow time for sufficient focus on personal and corporate renewal.

Let them know the pastor will be addressing some of the issues identified by leadership. I suggest that you pull your true intercessors together for a special prayer assignment. Ask them to pray that God will send a genuine spirit of conviction, repentance, and reconciliation. It would be helpful to schedule several special prayer meetings before the final Solemn Assembly.

8. *Preach a series focusing on personal and corporate renewal and revival.*

The climax of the series will be the Solemn Assembly. A series might include some of the following topics:

- A biblical pattern of a local church, Acts 2.
- A biblical profile of church leadership, 1 Timothy 3, Titus 1.
- The redemptive implications of a unified church, John 17.
- What God says about sin and repentance.
- Achans in the church, Joshua 7.
- The wages of sin.
- Letters to the Seven Churches of Asia Minor, Revelation 1-3.

9. *Turn the negatives, the sins, the shortcomings into positive goals for the future of the church.*

These items become your strategic objectives on the "other side" of the Solemn Assembly. Let the people know that their church can become, by God's grace,

a lighthouse to the lost.

a community of those who love each other.

a united body.

a fellowship that takes sin seriously.

a group noted for their cooperation with other believers.

a church which rises above denominationalism.

a family that prays for God's blessing upon other ministries.

a shelter for the hurting.

a healing community.

an authentic, transparent fellowship.

an accountable family.

10. Ask the parishioners to ask God to search their own hearts and respond appropriately.

The five to six weeks leading up to the assembly should be a period of prayer, confession, and reconciliation. Keep in front of them that on the day of the Solemn Assembly, a service of a "new beginning," a communion service, will be served and it is important that all examine themselves before partaking. Continually remind them that it is crucial that all the church family be present for the Solemn Assembly.

11. The final week before the assembly, have several seasons of prayer.

A special midweek prayer session, a time of prayer on Saturday, and several morning prayer meetings may be appropriate. The subject is the revival of the church. It's also a time of "plowing" hard soil. Churches have been known to ask their parishioners to actually write out their personal sins that need to be repented of and relationships that need to be reconciled.

12. The Solemn Assembly will have to be "custom made," because each church family is different.

Still, there are several components that probably should be present. Normal schedules should be set aside. An hour service just won't do it. The people during Hezekiah's time spent fourteen days in God's presence. Obviously, that's not an option today. It does, however, help us understand that a normal service probably isn't adequate. I suggest that at least three hours be set aside for the Assembly.

God's Word is a vital, powerful, convicting element in the Solemn Assembly. It brought about a revival under Ezra and Josiah. It is indeed living and powerful. Depending on church size and church custom, it is good to have a lot of Scripture read, especially those which focus on the grandeur, the holiness, the majesty of God. My preference would be to ask parishioners to choose and read the Scriptures. If this is not possible, elders or deacons could be assigned ahead of time to read such passages as Isaiah 6, Revelation 4-5, etc.

Songs and Scripture should work together to lift the congregation into God's presence. I suggest at least fifteen to twenty songs be sung at the beginning. These could be interspersed with supporting Scriptures. As people hear of his majesty and sing about it, their hearts are softened to the things of God.

Confession is certainly an essential component. It is usually the fruit of adoration and worship. When we "see the Lord, high and lifted up," we find ourselves on our faces before Him. The pastor and leaders may need to lead the way. After one Prayer Summit, a pastor confessed his prayerlessness, his divisive spirit and his failures as a shepherd. He gave an altar call, walked down the aisle, turned and walked up the aisle in response to his own call. Almost forty joined him in confessing their own sin.

There are some good ways in which people can be encouraged to do business with God. People can be asked to write out those sins that the Spirit brings to mind. If this is done, the people should be told not to put their names on the list. Turned in, selective lists can be read with solemnity and contrition. Fifteen to twenty minutes of rehearsing such sin will encourage brokenness before God and set the stage for corporate and individual repentance. There is a point at which the rehearsing of sin creates a God-given anger, a hatred of all that is soiled, wrong, and impure.

The goal is that those prompted to pray will begin to

confess and renounce corporate and individual sins. If the church is small enough, church members should be encouraged to pray as the Lord prompts them. A large church may select a "choir loft" full of people prepared to pray for the church and its people. Certainly time should be given for personal reflection, personal confession, and brokenness before God.

During part of the service it may be beneficial to break the congregation into groups of three or four and lead them through group prayers of confession and repentance. Leaders should be prepared to ask people to seek reconciliation when it is appropriate. Again, the goal is to plan, yet let the Spirit of God orchestrate the time together.

The spirit of the occasion is that this is a service of "new beginning." Communion is the visible, tangible evidence of this new beginning. It is also a point of leverage as parishioners are encouraged to examine themselves and come clean with God and people. I suggest that a new church covenant be drawn up, one that declares the intentions of the people and calls them to action. If for some reason there does not seem to be a genuine spirit of humility, a willingness to deal with sin, I'd recommend you not serve communion, even though it is ready to be dispensed.

It is likely communion will be a wonderful climax and a joyous new beginning. Following communion, it could be appropriate to read the new church covenant as a declaration of solidarity and obedience. Close the Solemn Assembly with songs of joy and deliverance, songs that speak of cleansing and forgiveness, songs of commission. Plan the next Sunday service as a joyous celebration.

As a safeguard against decline, establish the habit of taking elders and deacons away for prolonged prayer and worship at least twice each year. Their unity is a must. It attracts the blessing of God.

Solemn Assemblies are sometimes necessary and are therefore good. But don't make a practice of having to call them! If you safeguard the ongoing ministry of your church by continual evaluation and fostering seasons of brokenness before God, they will not be common occurrences.

Radical surgery is sometimes necessary to save the body, but if you undergo it too often you won't have a body to save. Much better to take care of the body so it won't need radical surgery.

The same is true of your church. It is, after all, a body. So keep it healthy!

12

THE PRAYER SUMMIT
Where Reunitus Begins

Prayer Summits work.

Pastor Donald Roth attended a Prayer Summit in Cedar Springs, Washington and penned an article describing his experience. He writes:

> Our goal is not to talk about praying, but to pray; not to discuss God, but to meet with God; not to discuss man's agenda, but to seek God's agenda. Shouldn't Baptists and Presbyterians and Charismatics and Lutherans who love the same Lord come to love each other as brothers and sisters and as co-laborers with Christ?

> It was April 1989 in Portland, Oregon. The tear-streaked face of Dr. Joe Aldrich [President of Multnomah School of the Bible] communicated his brokenness, passion, and love for pastors.

> During the past year he had traveled up and down the West coast of the United States leading over twenty small interdenominational groups of pastors in four-day prayer retreats. The purpose was prayer—no program, no agenda, just prayer!

> Six months later in October 1990, thirty pastors—

six of whom were Canadians—representing several denominations, met at Cedar Springs Christian Retreat Center in a small, intimate chapel. It was their first prayer retreat.

We began with Dr. Aldrich encouraging us to pray and worship, permitting God to set the agenda. Spontaneously different pastors led the group in prayer, a cappella singing of choruses and hymns, and reading of Scripture.

During those days we were to sing over two hundred times, read dozens of passages of Scripture, and sense God's presence in a way that few of us had ever experienced.

At the closing of the first full day of prayer, worship, and eating meals together, bonds of trust and camaraderie had formed among the men. Denominational distinctives did not surface during the entire time together, but a common love for the Savior did.

The next day began where day one ended—praise worship and singing. But that day a new dynamic was to emerge. Dr. Joe invited each of us individually to share with fellow pastors personal needs and struggles we were experiencing in our family life and ministries. With bonds of trust and love firmly established, pastor after pastor opened his heart: church splits, tensions with church board members, spiritual fatigue, discouragement, emotional and physical burnout, hurting children and wives, and more.

What became obvious was that these pastors were a weary group of spiritual warriors, each one bearing scars and carrying heavy loads of physical, spiritual and emotional baggage as a result of front-line battle with the enemy.

Empathetic hearts responded spontaneously as fellow pastors quietly gathered around the hurting pastor. Tears of compassion were shed with love, and acceptance was freely offered as they prayed for spiritual healing and renewal.

It was apparent that this experience was a first for most pastors. Loads were lifted, burdens were lightened and I was reminded of the Scripture: "Therefore confess your faults to one another, and pray for one another, so that you may be healed" (James 5:16, TLB).

The third day, renewed and refreshed pastors prayed for individual churches, board members, families, ministry friends, and that these flames of prayer power would spread.

The last evening was highlighted by two-and-a-half hours of worship and sharing the Lord's supper. Before the Lord and his fellow ministers, each man was served communion after reciting a recommitment to his personal call of ministry.

During those wonderful days, God did a work of grace and restoration in the lives of thirty pastors as passion for ministry was rekindled.

This account could be repeated dozens of times. If we truly seek him, he may be found! He is pleased when we seek him with our whole heart.

A few excerpts from multitudes of letters illustrate that regardless of the location, time or constituents, the results are uniformly the same.

I was prompted to complete a work God had begun in me at the Summit, but which I was not ready to let go of then. For years I have held my associate in judgment and today I released him, asking his forgiveness. The brothers prayed for a rooting out of pride and selfishness in me. I now feel a greater freedom and love toward George than I ever have. That's what this is all about, isn't it?

A North Idaho pastor

It is hard for me to know how to express in a letter what the Prayer Summit . . . meant to me. You might remember me with the Salem pastors' Group. I was the one who cried for two days. God has been very gracious to me during this time. He has granted me the privilege of experiencing brokenness before him. I never knew how precious that could be. I am learning the freedom that comes from brokenness.

A Salem, Oregon pastor

The move of God was so deep and so great I felt reluctant to participate in the vocalizing of prayers because it was evident to me that such a holy thing was taking place it should not be entered into and participated in lightly.

An Aloha, Oregon pastor

What is a Prayer Summit?

Quite simply, a Prayer Summit is a gathering of Christian leaders designed to spend several days seeking the Lord and his agenda for their local community. It is a group of spiritual leaders who take seriously their responsibility to corporately prepare a community for an outpouring of God's blessing. But it's much more!

It's a prolonged prayer and praise meeting at which pastors from the same community discover their oneness in Christ.

It's a pastoral melting pot.

It's a regionally-focused prayer strategy to recover and demonstrate unity and thereby activate the evangelistic potential of John 17.

It's an environment where personal revival is common.

It's a time for repentance and reconciliation.

It's a time where God links pastors in common cause.

It's a great time of vision-stretching as united pastors take a fresh look at their community.

It's a time of spiritual warfare as Christian leaders are led to deal with personal and corporate sin.

It's a time of doing battle for a city.

It's the beginning of unprecedented cooperation and joint ministry.

It's the first phase in bringing revival to a whole church and community.

It's the precursor to a church-wide Solemn Assembly.

What Makes a Prayer Summit Work?

Why do they work? Because extended time in God's presence changes things. In fact, its the only thing I know of that has a chance of bringing together born-again representatives of great ecclesiastical diversity in genuine corporate fellowship.

Pastoral conferences won't do it. Workshops won't do it. Commissions on unity and ecumenism won't do it.

Only a powerful, sustained time in His presence will tear down ancient walls, build bonds of love, and link brothers in common cause.

When two separated brethren find themselves at the feet of Jesus, at the foot of the same cross, the distance between them shrinks to almost nothing. As they worship together, weep together, and minister together, things change. Caricatures are eliminated, issues are brought into balance, and hearts are knit in common cause.

As pastors humble themselves before God and each other and allow others to minister to them, unity is inevitable. Each sees the other in an entirely new light . . . as broken people . . . as wounded soldiers . . . as discouraged pastors . . . as needy people . . . as brothers indeed.

Imagine singing seventy-five to one hundred songs a day for four days! Words can't describe the worship, the two-hour communion services, the prayers and reading of Scripture, the extended times of complete silence before God. Then add to that the times of laying on of hands and praying for each other and the deliverances from sin and its bondage.

The lessons learned about openness, transparency, and authenticity alone will reshape whole ministries. Clergy invite other clergy into their lives as instruments of ministry and deliverance. A new vision of worship is marking many churches.

At every Prayer Summit there is forgiveness and reconciliation. Pastors embrace pastors with tears coursing down their cheeks. There is great joy and laughter that knows no bounds.

Why does it work? Because all the things that need to happen, happen. When God controls the agenda, when the Holy Spirit orchestrates the time together, nothing is missing, nothing is left out, nothing is overlooked.

What are the Components of a Prayer Summit?

Successful Prayer Summits all seem to have at least twelve common components. Let's take a look at them one by one.

1. There are no hidden agendas.

The Prayer Summit is not a platform for ministries to recruit for their causes. Truly, the only agenda is to meet with God. No books are sold, no albums made available, no speakers speak, no musicians perform. One pastor writes:

> ... The [leadership] helped us experience a significant moving of the Spirit of God without ever themselves becoming the focus of attention.

> It was like going to a conference with Jesus as the guest speaker. It would be difficult to overstate the significance of this event and others like it in the Northwest.

In a very real sense, leaders don't know what will happen the next hour. I well remember our first Prayer Summit held at the Cannon Beach Conference Center on the Oregon coast. Believe me, we were cruising uncharted waters. To our amazement, fifty-five pastors from Salem showed up—all, I am sure, skeptical about the whole idea. I guess I was foolish enough to risk it because of some valuable past experiences with small groups.

While at Dallas Theological Seminary I taught Group Dynamics for a couple of years. I was familiar with the components of a successful group experience. Four days of prayer and worship from morning to night, however, was a horse of a different wheelbase.

After a surprisingly wonderful first day, I turned to

Terry Dirks, one of the team members, and said, "Terry, we've got three more days. What in the world are we going to do?" We decided to stick with the original plan and let God control our time together. The rest is history!

2. *The Holy Spirit orchestrates the time together.*

We're not dealing with rookies. These leaders are veterans who desire nothing more than to meet with God. The time is fluid and free-flowing. One pastor leads in a prayer that prompts another to start a song which prompts another to read a Scripture or pray or sing or express a thought. About the only fixed items in the schedule are the meals, though we have worshiped and prayed our way through several of them.

3. *The participants represent nearly every church fellowship.*

There is a faithful remnant to be found in just about every denomination. The goal of a Prayer Summit is not to bring together conservatives and liberals. Like oil and water, they don't mix.

Nor is it to get denominational leaders talking. The goal is to link grass-root shepherds with grass-root, Bible-believing, God-honoring shepherds, regardless of their church affiliations. The goal is to provide an environment which melts them and fuses them as one. And it happens.

I remember one pastor from a separatist fellowship who asked forgiveness for his denominational arrogance and acknowledged that he now believed the others in attendance were his true brothers in Christ. Sadly, he went on to say that he could not continue to meet with the men when they returned home. He would be censored for such association.

4. *The participants come from the same geographical area.*

There is a reason for this. We want people to go back as united brothers to the same neighborhood. We want them to know the pastors in the churches they drive past every day. We do not want them to disperse to the four winds. Our desire is that they continue to pray, worship, and strategize together. Dozens of groups meet weekly as a result of the Summits.

5. *The participants are significantly bonded to each other.*

Relationships do continue after the Summit. Pulpit exchanges take place. Regular, joint evening services are held. Prayer concerts are not uncommon. Salem, Oregon has had three to four corporate meetings averaging over 3,000 in attendance. Portland had a corporate gathering titled "An Evening of Joy" with 13,500 people in attendance. A number of areas have sponsored elder/deacon seminars. Several churches have taken their elders away for Prayer Summits. One church has taken several large groups of parishioners on a prayer retreat.

6. *Prayer Summits involve people of the same sex.*

We discovered that the men are not nearly as apt to open up and express their heartfelt concerns if women are present. Some struggle with pornography. Not a few need deliverance from sexual abuse in their childhoods. Though this is not a hard and fast rule, we have found it best to separate the sexes and provide separate Summits for men and women. Incidentally, the women we've dealt with prefer to have their own Summits.

7. *Next to meeting with God, a second purpose of the summit is to seek God's plan for impacting a specific geographical area with the gospel.*

A caution: We Westerners move toward the programmatic too quickly. Still, we desire pastors and leaders to go back to their community with their eyes opened to the power of tactical unity. We desire that they continue to worship, pray, communicate, and reach out together.

Ultimately, we believe God is leading the church back to John 17 so that the world may know that God loves them. Therefore the "Church of Salem" must roll up its sleeves and begin to pray and plan to mount a sustained effort to influence the city.

The emphasis must not be on "taking" a city. That implies a decisive, once-and-for-all victory that is not likely because the battle for cities will rage until the Lord returns. The goal is not an "event" in which we spiritually map a city and then take it. The goal is to sustain successful warfare until the Lord returns—a much more difficult challenge than an event-centered operation. Difficult because in our "instant everything" culture, we are not used to long sieges. A "now or nothing" mentality won't cut it.

Please don't misunderstand me. Mass public events are part of the program, but they are just that—*one part* of a sustained, ongoing strategy to move as a unified army until the Lord returns. Each individual church where Christ is honored must see itself as part of a bigger whole. We've violated the truth of John 17 for too long!

8. *Each Prayer Summit ends with a unique covenant.*

These covenants are unique in the sense that each group constructs a description of what their unity will look like when they leave.

Each group has committed itself to meet on a regular basis. Each has committed to gather again for another Prayer Summit. Many agree that they will never again undercut other ministries or speak ill of their brothers in

Christ. Some have set up quarterly Prayer Summits where they spend a day together in worship and prayer. Some groups agree to join as couples for an evening of food and fellowship. The first time the Vancouver, Washington group met, they had eighty men and women in attendance.

9. *The Prayer Summit is the "engine" of revival for a local church and its surrounding community.*

"How many of you," I asked a Prayer Summit group, "actually believe God is going to bring revival to your church? To your city?" Even after some coaxing, not a pastor raised his hand. What we see—our expectations—is usually what we get. Part of faith is visualizing something beforehand and then acting in concert with its realization. As the pastors realize they are not alone, that their fellowship need not be limited to their "own brand," that corporately they can impact a city, faith builds and vision returns.

Salem, Oregon pastors believe that when revival starts in the Northwest, it will begin in their town. The way they're going, that's a great possibility.

10. *Prayer Summits are painful and traumatic.*

Divine surgery is often excruciating and humiliating. It hurts to heal. At the proper time a "hated chair" is put into the center of the circle and those who need prayer, forgiveness, deliverance, and healing are invited to sit in the chair and bare their hearts. As one dear pastor said, "I've wept more in the last four days than in my lifetime." Yes, friend, pastors are hurting people. When they are assured they have found a safe environment, a setting where they can be sheep rather than shepherds, they flock to the chair.

Inevitably, when the session with the chair ends,

pastors approach us asking if the chair can be put out again because they want an opportunity to be prayed for. One church leader resisted the heavy hand upon him for three days. The last night he wrestled with God and finally agreed to deal with the sin in his life the final morning. In a letter written to me he proclaimed that "I will never be the same again."

As burdens are shared, as sins are confessed, as relationships are healed, the pastor on the chair is surrounded by volunteers who come to lay their hands on him and pray. Often they come because they are struggling with the same issues.

A mainline pastor sobbed as he poured out his broken heart. His daughter had taken to the streets. They hadn't heard from her for months. He was bitter toward God. His ministry was at a standstill. I was touched as pastors hurried to his side, laid their hands on him, and stormed the courts of heaven on his behalf. I was especially touched to see Baptists and Charismatics praying together for this brother.

11. A Prayer Summit isn't limited to pastors.

As I mentioned previously, when I was in the pastorate, I took my board away on similar prayer retreats. All church business was left behind. Our only agenda was to be in his presence and seek his will for our church and community. Some churches are taking groups from their congregation away for their own Prayer Summits. If I were back in the pastorate, it would be a must.

12. A Prayer Summit should involve at least one-third of the leaders of a given evangelical church community.

We call this a "critical mass." If one-third of the evangelical community leaders are meeting together for four days of prayer, they have enough people involved to carry on the momentum when they return.

That covers the twelve main components of a Prayer Summit. But what is involved in launching a Prayer Summit? We'll look at that next.

13.
LAUNCHING THE SHIP:
Guidelines for a Successful Prayer Summit

Archie Bunker and his son-in-law Meathead were having a theological discussion. As usual, Archie had the last word:

> He [God] made everyone the same religion . . . Christian, which he named after his son, Christian . . . or Christ for short. And that's how it was for years. One religion until they started splitting them up into all them denumerations. But there's still only one religion: His up there.

For once in his life, Archie was right. It's one thing, however, to analyze a problem; it's something else to bring those "denumerations" together.

Perhaps God is calling you to be part of the solution. Could it be that he would want you to be the "Hezekiah" of your community? You're convinced that John 17 is not merely divine rhetoric. You have a great burden to see the church become one in your community and accomplish its redemptive mission. So where do you go from here?

Perhaps you feel like the Lone Ranger, or Elijah. I'll start out by reminding you that Elijah's perception was wrong. He wasn't the "last of the Mohicans," or the "lone stranger." There were, in fact, more than seven thousand others who shared his theological commitments. I've observed that the Lord is raising up people of like passion from all over the country.

People who have a heart for revival.

People who are bridge-builders.

People who are men and women of prayer.

People who long to see the true Body become one in mission and purpose.

People like you . . . .

If you're convinced a Prayer Summit could be God's desire for your community, where do you begin? Let me give you some suggestions.

How to Start a Prayer Summit

I have no divine lock on how to run a successful Prayer Summit, but I have had some valuable experience in that arena. The following guidelines come out of that experience.

1. Assemble a core of interested Christian leaders.

Become a seed-planter. On a one-to-one basis begin to talk about the possibility of getting together with a group of local leaders to seek the presence of God and discover his agenda for your community. You need not be a pastor! Many laymen have been involved in Prayer Summits. These interested leaders should have several characteristics. They should be:

- believers, committed followers of Jesus Christ.
- representative of the broader Christian traditions.
- burdened for revival.
- men and women of prayer.

- free of scandal.
- respected by the Christian community.
- leaders in their own denominations.
- willing to risk.
- charismatic and non-charismatic.
- bridge-builders.

2. Secure a respected, well-accepted leader to convene the Prayer Summit.

This leader should be known as a bridge-builder. Usually there is someone in each community who is trusted and highly respected. It could be a layman or a staff member of a parachurch ministry. Most likely he will not be a novice or new to the community. If the Prayer Summit is perceived as "owned" by either charismatic or non-charismatic elements, it will be hard to "sell."

Remember Hezekiah. Though he was ridiculed for the idea, this twenty-five-year-old novice king convened one of history's greatest Prayer Summits.

3. Assemble a well-respected leadership team.

Although one person may have more visibility than the others, it is best for the Summit to be "sponsored" by a group of five to six pastors who represent different theological traditions. I would also look for those who are in it for the long term, who have a persistent vision of seeing a community impacted for Christ. These leaders make up the core.

It is best that a Prayer Summit not be sponsored by a local ministerial association. If sponsorship grows out of a charismatic ministerial fellowship, for example, non-charismatics probably won't show up.

4. The concept must be sold to local pastors.

The vision must be communicated. After a core has

committed themselves to the concept, the idea needs exposure to the broader evangelical community. A breakfast meeting is often a good platform for sharing the vision. The goal is to discover, initiate, and sustain a comprehensive, inclusive work of God in your community. This vision has many components.

- A sustained work of God in your community.
- Community-wide growth of the body.
- Activation of the John 17 paradigm.
- Experience of a divinely orchestrated unity.
- Fine-tuning of the community to attract the blessing of God.
- Experience of a corporate sense of mission.
- Release of the corporate body to bring other ministries to health.
- Corporate renewal.
- A search for the remnant.
- Cooperation.
- Community worship and celebration events.

Remind these key leaders that unity is a biblical idea, that Satan attacked and destroyed the unity of Israel and is the enemy of unity in the Church. ("Protect them from the evil one, so that they may be one.")

Furthermore, throughout history God has raised up men and women to call the Church to repentance and renewal. Old Testament reformers called Solemn Assemblies. The Church used to as well. Thus the idea of a Prayer Summit is neither new nor unique.

I would communicate to them some idea of what to expect at a Prayer Summit. Assure them that hundreds have "taken the risk." Perhaps it would be good to thumb through this book and jot down some of the testimonies of pastors who have attended previous summits.

There's nothing like a satisfied customer.

It would be helpful to anticipate what their fears might be and try to address them. For most, it's a scary experience to commit themselves to live in close proximity with Christian leaders from diverse backgrounds. We have discovered that a no-host breakfast is a good place to begin communicating the vision. I would suggest you hand out a questionnaire to determine interest and provide you with follow-up materials.

Be persistent. Follow up with phone calls. If necessary, a little peer pressure works wonders. We asked a local Christian radio station to suggest that parishioners ask their pastors or leaders if they plan to attend the Summit. Believe me, it works.

5. *Locate and book some facilities.*

If a third of the evangelical community has expressed a desire to participate, it's time to secure a location for the Summit. Some facility suggestions:

- The retreat center should be within a reasonable distance of "home base."
- Try to avoid "church camps" with bath-house and bunk beds.
- It should be conducive to worship. Traffic noise, the "hustle and bustle of life" should be noticeably absent. A nature setting is preferable.
- It should provide good food service and dining facilities. Much happens at mealtime. The aesthetics are important.
- Negotiate a reasonable price. It may help to raise some scholarship funds from interested churches and individuals.

Continue recruiting until the last day. Many sign on at the last minute.

6. Prepare and mail some pre-Summit instructions.
These instructions should include such items as:

- how to get there.
- what to wear.
- sleeping provisions.
- what to bring, what not to bring.
- starting and finishing times.
- expectations.
- who is included.

We have toyed with alternatives to a Monday-Thursday format, but shorter versions have not proven as effective and lasting.

7. Make arrangements for transportation.

Your goal is to have all the participants go together rather than drive their own vehicles. Pastors are notorious for coming late and leaving early. A rented bus or a church bus will suffice. Having them change seats every twenty minutes helps them get acquainted. If possible, a brunch on the way to the retreat center accelerates the networking process.

8. The Summit should contain both charismatics and non-charismatics, mainline and independents.

Strive for a good cross-section of the evangelical community. Least valuable would be to gather with only your own group or denomination.

I'm not a charismatic. I've not spoken in tongues, I don't have any desire to, and I'm not seeking the experience. However, I often speak in charismatic circles and enjoy rich fellowship with these delightful brothers and sisters. While nature seems to dictate that "birds of a feather flock together," that is not the mandate for the Body of Christ.

Diversity must be joined with diversity if Christ is the

head of both. Against tradition, against common sense, Methodist "sparrows" may have to share their nests with Presbyterian "robins" and Lutheran "canaries" if the local community is to be impacted by Christ, the head of the "flock." Even if a pigeon flies the coop and ends up with a flock of turkeys.

9. *Assign responsibility for registration.*

This is a critical role. Often the tone for the whole retreat is set by this person. He is responsible for room assignments, collecting of funds, and providing participants with a packet of materials (which would include a schedule, pamphlets about the retreat center, and a list of the names and addresses of the participants as well as a personal note of welcome). The registrar is usually the first to welcome the registrants. It helps to have an outgoing, warm, hospitable person fill this role.

We've found it helpful to assign roommates. Preferably, put folks together who don't know each other or are from a different church background. It's a stretching experience!

10. *Appoint a listening team.*

Because the program is unstructured and free-flowing, it is important to have a sense of what the Spirit is doing. The listening team's (three to four leaders) task is to be the "eyes and ears" for the group. They confer regularly with the leader to help him discern the Spirit's agenda. They should be sensitive to the participation profile, paying attention to those who don't join in or who tend to dominate. Usually the listening team meets each evening after the last session for evaluation and prayer.

11. *Arrange the room so that interaction is made as simple as possible.*

The best arrangement is probably a circle. Be sensitive to such things as lighting, heat, and noise. It's good to have a member of the listening team sit next to the group leader. This way they can be in communication without disrupting the group.

What Do We Do at the Retreat Center?

Let's assume that at this point you are at the retreat center and ready to roll. What's next?

Guidelines! The participants need some basic instructions that will set the stage for their time together. There are several things to be considered.

1. Participants should be sensitized to the varying traditions of worship represented in the room.

Some are used to all praying at once, others pray one at a time. Some would normally speak in tongues, others would not. Some are more comfortable in a liturgical environment, others are more casual in their worship. Some are vigorous and fervent in their prayers, others are more pensive and subdued. There are those who affirm another's prayers with a sort of verbal commentary as they "second" the prayer and encourage God to "do it." When asked to be considerate of other traditions, participants do just great. On only one occasion do I remember a group "taking off" and having to be reminded again of possible offense.

2. Participants need an explanation of the basic components of the Prayer Summit.

A Prayer Summit is composed of four basic elements. These include prayer, singing, the reading of Scripture, and personal response. There are no scheduled speakers. However, there are "teachable moments" when the leader or some other designated person may comment appropriately for ten to fifteen minutes. In one Summit, a pastor was describing some serious problems on his home front. Dr. Howard Hendricks happened to be present. I asked him if he'd take fifteen to twenty minutes to talk to us about marriage. We hung on every word, particularly in light of the hurting pastor and his needs.

Singing is a vital dynamic in the Summit process. On a given day, seventy-five to one hundred songs will be sung. There is no structured list of songs; they simply grow out of the flow of the prayer and reflection. I strongly suggest no instruments be used. There is nothing more powerful than voices singing in beautiful harmony—a harmony, by the way, which is often masked by a piano.

As a general rule, something is lost when you use a pianist or a song leader. Song leaders are wonderful for church services, but can actually hinder the flow of a Prayer Summit and take the focus off the Lord. In this special environment, a pre-planned list of songs takes away from the spirit of spontaneity.

I usually begin a Summit by asking participants to take five to ten minutes to jot down several passages that talk about the wonder and majesty of God. Then I ask several to "establish the perimeters" (more on that in a moment). I ask them to pray that God would protect us all from the evil one and his hosts. I also invite several to ask God to meet with us in a singular, significant, life-changing manner.

Following those initial requests, we usually shift our focus to center on the greatness of God. Scripture is used to sharpen our focus and direct our prayers. We literally turn Scripture into prayer. Someone will read Isaiah 6. Another will spontaneously start singing "Holy, Holy, Holy." "Thou Art Worthy" often grows out of the reading of Revelation 4-5. Prayers focus on the wonder and majesty of our God. This focus may hold for several hours.

This lifting up and exaltation of God inevitably brings great rejoicing and an increased sensitivity to sin. As God begins to reveal his presence, spiritual shoes come off. The ground is holy. The songs become more intense and meaningful. They gradually shift to the Cross and the wonders of our deliverance from sin. Tears start flowing. Confession begins. At first it's general and generic and impersonal. As emotional ice begins to thaw, as the Spirit prompts, the confession, the worship, the adoration becomes personal, genuine, and life-changing.

Don't be surprised if folks fall to their knees or prostrate themselves on the carpet. Some will stand, many will raise their hands in worship.

3. *Participants should receive instructions concerning the first communion service to be held later that evening.*

Challenge them to be certain that they are prepared to partake in a worthy manner. Of all people, Christian leaders should know the importance of a prepared heart, a good conscience before God and man. It might be that the Spirit would prompt you to spend the last hour before dinner preparing for communion.

As we approached our first communion with one group, a pastor stood and said, "I don't think any of us should take communion. We've sinned against each other, we've talked against each other's ministries." And he was right! This began an almost two-hour time of making things right. The communion service that followed was nothing short of glorious.

4. *Don't try in any way to force confession or reconciliation.*

These things will happen at the proper time. Sometimes it's well into the second day before hearts open up and healing begins to take place. As soon as a participant begins to reveal his burdened heart, encourage three to four pastors or leaders to surround the brother and lay their hands on him and lift him in prayer to the Father. These are precious, sacred moments. Moments never to be forgotten. Moments that words cannot describe. Moments with lasting impact. They're wall-shattering. Suddenly, labels make no difference.

5. *Don't be afraid of silence.*

Expect to have times when you're not sure where the group is going or what should happen next. You must believe that God has an agenda and that he's not trying to hide it, even though we don't always perceive his workings. I'll have to admit it gets scary at times.

6. *Influence the group's direction by reading specific passages that focus thoughts and prayers in an appropriate direction.*

For example, if you want to have them reflect on their lost Jerusalems with walls down and gates burned, begin reading from Nehemiah, chapter one. Imagine the group sitting with eyes closed as you read a few verses at a time and then wait for their response.

You read that Nehemiah fasted, prayed, and wept for days after hearing of Jerusalem's plight. You stop. There is silence. Then someone begins to pray. "Forgive me, Lord, I've never fasted, I've never wept over my Jerusalem." You continue reading and reach the section where Nehemiah confesses his sins, and you stop and wait for a Spirit-prompted response. Chances are good that person after person will begin to seek reconciliation with God and man.

Another meaningful exercise is to pray through Joshua 5 and 6, asking the Lord to prompt insights concerning how to take a city. It's amazing how effective a prayer/instructional time can be. God does indeed prompt insights relevant to the battle for our cities.

If the focus shifts to family, Ephesians 5 and 6 would be appropriate. This will give direction and focus to their prayers.

7. *Be sensitive to time.*

Try not to run on an hourly, predictable schedule. It's more than likely you'll average an hour and a half per session, sometimes more. Time does, however, get away from you. On one occasion we sent the men out six at a time for a "beach walk." It was a wonderful sight to see groups of six walking down the beach, arms around each other, singing at the top of their voices. We all gathered in a natural amphitheater at Haystack Rock and had a spontaneous worship service. Over fifty men sang their hearts out . . . right through the lunch hour.

8. *As the Lord leads, provide participants with some personal time where they can be alone with God.*

Often they need time to debrief, to reflect, and to deal with some personal agendas. We usually provide them with an hour or more each afternoon for "solitary time." In this regard, it is sometimes appropriate to ask them to maintain a "discipline of silence."

9. *Occasionally it is entirely appropriate to break participants into small groups for a short time.*

We often break the larger group into groups of five or six and ask them to find a spot where they will feel comfortable to pray. It would be typical to find them in dorm rooms and other nooks and crannies. If the weather allows, they will be outside.

The Lord may prompt you to suggest they complete a written assignment. On one occasion the Lord directed us to have the men write out their vows to God. At communion time, each man repeated his vows to God with their brothers serving as supporters and witnesses. Those were precious moments of consecration and renewal.

10. Provide opportunities for participants to publicly declare their love for God.

Make it clear that you are not asking them to tell you why they love the Lord. They are to tell their Lord why they love him, and let their peers have the privilege of listening in on the conversation. Usually I put a chair in the center of the circle and suggest that Christ is sitting there. Participants are invited to come and kneel before the chair and verbalize their love of the Lord.

It's a wonderful experience.

11. Use the "Perimeters of Control" as a general guideline for the group process.

There are several "defense perimeters" that must be repaired and maintained if the individual believer is to maintain spiritual health and stamina. Satan surely is attacking each of these arenas or battlefields. The flow of the Summit often proceeds along these lines.

The first perimeter is the individual and his relationship to God. If that is weak, Satan has access to all the other perimeters. Most of the prayer at the beginning of the summit seems to focus on one's relationship with God. Much of the "healing" at the Prayer Summits take place at this level.

The second perimeter is the pastor's relationship with his wife. Here we usually encounter great areas of weakness. Pastor's wives are the walking wounded, often sacrificed on the altar of ministry. I remember so well a dear brother pouring out his heart over the state of his marriage. His wife was chronically depressed and suicidal. We surrounded this dear brother and lifted him and his wife into the hands of the Great Physician. At a dinner three weeks later she told the pastors how God had wonderfully healed her on the very day we had prayed for her.

When you sense prayers beginning to focus in this area, it is often prudent to reinforce the emphasis by reading from passages relating to husbands and wives. Let Scripture direct their prayers!

The third perimeter of control is the family. Certainly the wise pastor puts the concerns of his family ahead of the concerns of the congregation. Many pastors are burdened by children out of control or in need of a special touch from the Lord. Oceans of tears are shed over concerns of marriage and family. Many are devastated by prodigal kids. Bitterness toward God for his seeming lack of concern is not uncommon. A Prayer Summit provides the environment to deal with these heavy, heartbreaking issues.

The fourth perimeter of control is the church board or governing body. A pastor is foolish to attempt to correct congregational problems if he faces a divided, carnal leadership team. But politics, power-plays and seeds of discord abound in leadership teams. Satan knows he can neutralize a church by prevailing in any one of these perimeters of control.

The fifth perimeter of control is the church family. If the board and leadership are divided, the congregation will be ineffectual in living out the gospel. And God will not put healthy spiritual babes in an unhealthy spiritual environment. Churches with ongoing internal feuds will not receive the blessing of God. Satan knows that and keeps the fires of division burning.

The final perimeter of control is the community. Generally speaking, it is foolish to develop evangelism strategies if any or all of the other perimeters of control have been breached by the Evil One. The community needs to hear the beauty of the gospel played out through the lives of those who dwell together in unity. Genuine edification must precede evangelism.

The flow of a Prayer Summit seems to follow these perimeters of control. It is helpful to have them in mind so that you and the listening team can answer the question, "Where are we?" I should underscore, however, that seldom are two Summits the same.

12. Be a full participant yourself.

It is important that you, too, respond to the Spirit and share with others the gift of your need. It is inconceivable to me that you would not need to sit in the hated chair and let others minister to you in some area of your life.

13. If possible, use a leadership team approach.

We try to have a least two and preferably three leaders. While one may serve as a facilitator, he is in constant contact with the others. In fact, we always sit together so that we can converse quietly, if necessary, as the Summit unfolds. We are constantly asking such questions as:

Where are we?
What is the Spirit doing?
What is the area of need to which He is directing us?
What Scripture would reinforce direction?
Has the style of worship offended anyone?
When should we put out the chair?

Are the men tired?

Is it time to break into small groups?

Furthermore, the leaders are in constant touch between sessions, and meet each evening to pray and review the events of the day.

14. Prayer Summits are worth it.

Prayer Summits are marvelous tools to bring pastors in a local community back to obedience to the John 17 mandate. They are also excellent tools to bring healing and unity to local church boards and communities. An Episcopal pastor told me that the changed life of one of the pastors impacted his entire community.

Yes, lives are changed. A pastor's daughter wrote me the following note following her dad's attendance at a Prayer Summit. She wrote:

> When dad told me he was going to the Prayer Summit I got extremely excited for him and what I knew he would experience. He believes it was the most incredible four days of his life!
>
> He talked for hours about it when he got home and the change is REAL! His ministry has never been so real to him, his heart for the lost is burning deep within! His vision for the world has returned like never before.
>
> His sensitivity to my family is truly awesome. I love dad dearly and praise the Lord for the growing relationship we now have!
>
> I look at him and have to ask if this is the same man who has been my father for eighteen years! And I say no! What an answer to prayer.

Now, *that's* a testimony. You can't fool a teenager!

14.

WHERE DO WE GO FROM HERE?: The Power of Corporate Gathering

Is it worth it? Can Christian leaders in a given community, already swamped by overloaded schedules, band together and make a difference? Will God respond to their efforts to "come to complete unity"? C. Dale German, a Nazarene pastor, wrote the following article after participating in a unified worship service here in Portland, Oregon. His letter is not overstated. I was there.

THE SPIRIT OF PORTLAND

Intellectually I knew I was not alone in my love for Christ and my burden for the city of Portland. There is my family, my congregation, my Thursday pastor's fellowship. But living in a city where Christians are not respected and pastors are especially ridiculed, I "felt" alone.

Until this night. January 19, 1992.

This night over 13,500 Christians from every evangelical denomination dismissed their evening services. In buses, vans, and cars they came to fill the Portland Coliseum. The opening words of this historic worship and praise service were, "This is the best family reunion Portland has ever had."

To that, cheers and applause thundered across the vast auditorium. For the next 2 1/2 hours our spirits were one in Christ. The celebrating never let up. Together we sang and prayed and clapped for God.

All of us share the burden. All of us feel the spiritual oppression in Portland and the Northwest. All of us want to have the city of Portland shaken for God and righteousness.

Never has there been in Portland a unifying force as this one was. With minimum human leadership, our focus was totally on God and his son, Jesus Christ. In unity people freely worshiped in their own unique ways. Some stood and sang with hands raised to the heavens, while others sat quiet with heads bowed. Occasionally the whole crowd felt the same thing at the same time and unanimously burst out in applause or expressed its agreement by standing.

Over 13,500 people wrote down a total of more than 90,000 names of men and women they wanted to see won to Christ in Portland and committed themselves to pray toward that end. Those names were collected, taken to the platform and dumped like a Niagara Falls at the foot of a big, wooden cross. As the vast crowd united in prayer for those names, leaders on the platform knelt in a circle around the cross and the mound of names, and placed the names before the throne of God in prayer.

Earlier we were instructed to break into little groups of no more than four and pray together. Our prayer was to be simple. We invited God to come to the city of Portland. What a sight to see 2,500 prayer cells petitioning God to come to Portland.

Though Billy Graham is coming to Portland in September, the Graham Crusade had nothing official to do with this gathering. We were simply a gathering of believers joined together to see how strong we really are in number and spirit. Our only desire was to celebrate the glory of God and rejoice in our common salvation.

As I worshiped amidst the atmosphere of people singing and clapping and raising holy hands, the following thoughts came to me.

Our leader is Jesus Christ.
Our power is prayer.
Our weapon is the Bible.
Our strength is in our numbers.
We are a mighty army of God.

We are the church and we are marching in Portland to conquer this city for him.

We will not win this city with anger.
We will not storm Portland by shouting.
We will penetrate the darkness of moral night with humble brokenness

person by person
heart by heart
and soul by soul, in love preferring one another.

We will lift up Jesus Christ and him only.
We will pray and sing and hold hands and open the windows of heaven by faith.
We will laugh.
We will rejoice.

We will be glad in the Lord and share our liberty
to everyone until all of Portland,

the politicians,
the media,
the homeless,
the drug addicts,
the homosexuals

cannot fail to hear that God loves us all alike.

Whomever we are.
Whatever we do.

And they will all hear that the blood of Jesus
Christ cleanses from all unrighteousness for he is
just the same yesterday, today, and forever.

We will love Jesus, for he alone is worthy to
receive power, and riches, and wisdom, and
strength, and honor, and glory, and blessing.

The celebration closed with a glorious surprise, the
memory of which this pastor will carry with him
until the day he dies. Every pastor was asked to
walk to the front of the auditorium, stand before
the cross, then turn and face the congregation.

No one anticipated what would happen next.

Uncounted hundreds of us came forward.

We who have been so scandalized by the media.
We who live in such loneliness of leadership.
We who in the world are made to feel so unwanted,
unappreciated.
We whom the world regards as so uninformed and
beside the point.

As we came out from the ranks of laymen and

began to mass before the people, all heaven broke loose. For the first time, all of us in the same instant saw how many of us there are. In a universal thunder of clapping, the whole place broke loose with long, sustained applause for Portland's pastors.

No walk down any aisle has ever meant more to me than this walk.

Intellectually, I knew I was not alone. But at 8:30 P.M. January 19, 1992, I saw that I was not alone. For the first time in my life, every fiber of my being FELT like I was not alone. All I could do was stand there with my fellow pastors before 13,500 Christians I will never know personally, thank God for Jesus and the power of his blood, and think of the reception that awaits all of us—for if angels rejoice when we are saved, they will surely applaud when we make it safely home to heaven.

As the crowd dispersed I sat down to write some final thoughts. By the time I was done the auditorium was almost empty. Billy Graham is coming in September. His beloved team member, George Beverly Shea, sometimes sings the words, "I'd rather have Jesus than man's applause."

The thought came to me: All of us who were there this night would rather have Jesus; but on this night when we gathered together with just one thought of praising God, He gave back to us the applause we offered to Him.

This is the new SPIRIT OF PORTLAND, and it is growing!

Ancient Israel was required to come to Jerusalem three times a year. We have overlooked the power and impact of these corporate gatherings as well as the power of their feasts. The Passover was the heart of their theology. It was a time for doing business with God, for settling accounts with God and man. It was a perpetual reminder of the basics of faith. It was a time of powerful worship, a time of reconciliation and restoration.

The psalms are full of "songs of ascent." These ancient hymns reflect the power and impact of doing something together, doing something big, doing something *en masse*. Is it any wonder that Jeroboam, the first king of the Northern kingdom, built rival temples to Jerusalem and refused to let his people return to that holy city? He cut the heart out of God's divine discipleship program.

The absence of the large, corporate gathering has weakened the church and kept it divided. We have discovered the value of such meetings and encourage each community to do at least one each year. The enthusiasm for this "Evening of Joy" (as we labeled our Portland event) is enormously gratifying. The benefits are manifold. Allow me to underscore some of them.

- Christians discover that they are not alone.
- Believers discover the great diversity in the Body and come to appreciate it.
- Caricatures are eliminated.
- Reconciliation takes place.
- God is truly worshiped.
- The exposure to different worship styles is most helpful.
- Bonds of love are formed.
- The people observe their pastor in association with others of like faith.

- The power and blessing of God is unleashed and flows out to the churches.
- People love it. So do pastors.

But not every corporate gathering will be successful. The following suggestions may be helpful as you pray about such an event.

1. Let such an event follow a Prayer Summit.

We encourage pastors to cancel their evening services the Sunday following a Prayer Summit. The pastors are joy-filled, rejuvenated, and bonded together. Almost half of the four hundred or so pastors who came forward at the "Evening of Joy" had just returned from a prayer Summit. We met an hour early with more than two hundred pastors and had an incredible time of worship and praise.

2. Don't feature "personalities" or celebrities of one kind or another.

Invite them to come and "meet with God." I suggest that no one be introduced all evening. Everyone on the program goes to the microphone unintroduced, completes their assignment, and is seated. Musicians sing, worship leaders lead without anyone's name being mentioned. The focus is on God, and God alone. People love it. It doesn't highlight any person or ministry.

3. Do it well.

There is no room for shoddiness in the Lord's work. Sound systems should be excellent. Seating should be adequate. If a band is used, they should rehearse. The worship leader should be well qualified and no one should remember who he is when the evening is over.

4. Select an adequate facility, preferably not a church.

Go to a civic auditorium-type facility. You will probably not have enough space available. Think big. Seventeen hundred more than planned for showed up in Kitsap

County, Washington. Double the anticipated amount showed up in Centralia, Washington. Several thousand more than we anticipated attended "An Evening of Joy." Many had to be turned away.

5. *Don't sponsor a "Corporate Gathering" until the pastors are bonded together.*

The biblical pattern is union, humility, unity, and community. Ideally, it's best to have some type of Prayer Summit before scheduling a gathering.

6. *Visualize the benefits.*

The blessing of God, his grace, will flow out from the gathering into each local church. Pastors regularly attest that they and their congregations are changed as a result of such events. Recently a pastor told me that his people were making frequent references to the changes in their lives. He was rejoicing because he'd never had so many phone calls from people wanting to volunteer to be involved in the ministry. Never underestimate the power of Corporate Gatherings.

7. *View the Corporate Gathering as a faith builder.*

They prove to be such. Seeing so many like-minded people praising God is a never-forgotten experience. It generates a new faith and excitement about the plan and purposes of God. It may generate a real sense of revival in your church. Often it opens people up to new methods of worship and praise.

8. *As a general rule, don't have any speakers.*

Break the time down into segments such as a time to:

- focus upon the greatness and majesty of God.
- focus upon the sinfulness of man.
- focus upon forgiveness and cleansing.
- focus upon the mission of the Christian in his world.

We followed that format for our first "Evening of Joy." Each segment was allotted about a half-hour. Selected pastors read Scripture, and in some cases commented on God's forgiveness and cleansing. Songs were interspersed throughout each of the segments.

9. Choose the worship leader carefully.

Avoid the grandiose, grandstand type leader. He should have a reputation for directing people to focus on God and him alone. Printed song sheets are helpful. I suggest you have no program listing events, songs, names, etc. Let it be a seamless affair that flows uninterrupted from start to finish.

10. Directed prayer can be an important component.

While this is true, I would not let it overpower singing and reading of Scripture. People don't want sermons, they want to meet with God. During "An Evening of Joy" we asked people to break up into groups of three or four and pray about some specific areas of need. One of the pastors led them through this exercise and it was quite effective.

11. Take an offering.

Make no pleas, twist no arms, play no tricks. If God's in it, he'll provide. We had twice as much money come in as was needed to cover all the expenses.

12. Rent a good sound system.

House systems are usually poor. It's better to be safe than sorry. At least have someone with expertise survey the situation and make recommendations. The Kitsap County Corporate Gathering was hindered by an inadequate sound system.

13. Use your creativity.

The worst method is the same method. Try to make the occasion as memorable as possible. Whatever leads participants into worship will fill the bill. Try to limit your program to two hours. Start and quit on time. It's better to leave them longing than loathing. Be sure the music director takes into account the fact that whenever he repeats a song, he eats up time. That's fine as long as the other parts of the program aren't jeopardized. Have a time schedule laid out and review it carefully with the program leaders.

14. Bathe it in prayer.

When God's people go to praying, all hell breaks loose. Satan's not happy with our prayers and will do all he can to disrupt and damage the cause of Christ.

May God enable us to get John 17 out of mothballs and into the mainstream of the life of the church.